Relationships That Work
(and Those That Don't)

≈

H. Norman Wright

Regal

A Division of Gospel Light
Ventura, California, U.S.A.

Published by Regal Books
A Division of Gospel Light
Ventura, California, U.S.A.
Printed in U.S.A.

Regal Books is a ministry of Gospel Light, an evangelical Christian publisher dedicated to serving the local church. We believe God's vision for Gospel Light is to provide church leaders with biblical, user-friendly materials that will help them evangelize, disciple and minister to children, youth and families.

It is our prayer that this Regal book will help you discover biblical truth for your own life and help you meet the needs of others. May God richly bless you.

For a free catalog of resources from Regal Books/Gospel Light please contact your Christian supplier or call 1-800-4-GOSPEL.

Cover Design by Barbara LeVan Fisher
Interior Design by Britt Rocchio
Edited by Ron Durham and David Webb

Library of Congress Cataloging-in-Publication Data
Wright, H. Norman.
    Relationships that work (and those that don't) / H. Norman Wright.
      p. cm.
    Includes bibliographical references.
    ISBN 0-8307-2198-3 (pbk.)
    1. Man-woman relationships. 2. Man-woman relationships—Religious aspects—Christianity.
3. Mate selection. 4. Mate selection—Religious aspects—Christianity. I. Title.
    HQ801.W843 1998
    306.7—dc21
    CIP
    98-15022

3 4 5 6 7 8 9 10 11 12 13 14 15 16 17 18 19 20 / 04 03 02 01 00

Rights for publishing this book in other languages are contracted by Gospel Literature International (GLINT). GLINT also provides technical help for the adaptation, translation and publishing of Bible study resources and books in scores of languages worldwide. For further information, contact GLINT, P.O. Box 4060, Ontario, CA 91761-1003, U.S.A., or the publisher.

Contents

≈

Introduction

≈

This book focuses on two major concerns that seem to plague many people today: identifying the positive potentials for a long-term relationship—and avoiding those relationships with incurable negatives. We might call this process, "How to Avoid Wasting Your Time, Energy and Money on a Hopeless Relationship."

One or two of the topics here are expanded from a previous book, *Finding Your Perfect Mate*, published by Harvest House. It would be helpful for you to read that book as well, since it also deals with many of the basic issues singles are concerned with today. They include learning whether marriage is for you or not, dealing with the fear of a relationship, what to do if you haven't recovered from a previous relationship, the reasons why you're still single, where to meet the opposite sex and what to say, how to get out of a bad relationship and getting married again.

That was a lot to cover in one book. Hence the need for the book you hold in your hands. The material presented here is based on more than 30 years of talking with those who are single, as well as those who are married. Hopefully this information will help you to develop and build your own quality, lifelong relationship.

The Wide, Wide World of Relationships

≈

Some people are "relationally homeless." They relate to others in a pattern that might be called "relational channel surfing"—switching from one relationship to another without staying with one long enough to connect.

Relationships are all around us. Everywhere. Commercials and TV programs are built on them. We think about them, talk about them and experience them. Well, perhaps the first two. Not all of us have experienced significant relationships, though we may want to. I'm not even sure many people know what is meant by the word. Some people are in *situations*, not relationships. (More on that later.)

Relationships are one of the most significant elements of life. We were created to be in relationships, not to exist without them. Most of our lives are spent in various relationships. Take them away, and our existence becomes sterile. Sure, there are those who appear not to need them, but they're the exceptions.

The Relationally "Homeless"

It's a sad fact of life that many people today are part of our society's homeless population. You know who the homeless are. You see them on street corners or in front of the post office. It's not uncommon to see a man or a woman dressed in shabby, dirty clothes standing on the sidewalk with a cardboard sign that reads, "Will work for food," or even a family living in an old car on a church parking lot. I've heard of couples who, unable to earn enough money to pay for a roof over their heads, move from home to home house-sitting or even skipping town before the rent is due. These people are the *visibly* homeless. But we have many today whose kind of homelessness is not so apparent. They are the *relationally* homeless.

Many single people suffer with this condition. Just as the physically homeless tend to drift, so do those who are relationally homeless. They're unable to find significant others to connect with, or they don't stay in any one relationship long enough to get to know or be known by another person. This jumping around or drifting pattern has been referred to as "relational channel surfing." That is, they hop from one relationship to another without ever making a commitment or staying long enough to connect.

Sometimes it's fear that keeps us from reaching out and connecting. It could be that closeness is too threatening, so we pull away. Or it could be that the "crop" of eligibles seems to be reflective of a farming community that recently experienced a drought! It's true that it's difficult for any single person today to find someone who is safe, sane and sanctified!

Sometimes being relationally homeless is not of our own making. It takes extra effort to find others, as well as an extra investment of time to cultivate positive relationships.[1]

Grounded in God

Relationships have their basis in the Bible. Isn't it interesting that the first statement God made concerning the man He created was, "Let us make man in our image" (Gen. 1:26)? Each of us was created to model our life and character on the image of God. But the God that we are to reflect is a God of relationships—Father, Son and Holy Spirit.

Then we read, "It is not good for the man to be alone" (Gen. 2:18). Loneliness is the first thing that God said was not good. The book of Ecclesiastes says:

> Two are better than one, because they have a good return for their work: If one falls down, his friend can help him up. But pity the man who falls and has no one to help him up! (4:9,10).

Max Lucado, in his own unique way, brings another perspective to relationships:

> A relationship. The delicate fusion of two human beings. The intricate weaving of two lives; two sets of moods, mentalities, and temperaments. Two intermingling hearts, both seeking solace and security.
>
> A relationship. It has more power than any nuclear bomb and more potential than any promising seed. Nothing will drive a man to greater courage than a relationship. Nothing will fire the heart of a patriot or purge the cynicism of a rebel like a relationship.
>
> What matters most in life is not what ladders we climb or what ownings we accumulate. What matters most is a relationship.
>
> What steps are you taking to protect your "possessions"? What means are you using to ensure that your relationships are strong and healthy? What are you doing to solidify the bridges between you and those in your world?
>
> Our Master knew the value of a relationship. It was through relationships that he changed the world. His movement thrived not on permission or power but on championing the value of a person. He built bridges and crossed them. Touching the leper...uniting the estranged...exalting

the prostitute. And what was that he said about loving your neighbor as yourself?

It's a wise man who values people above possessions.[2]

The "Mutualability" Factor

So, what is a relationship? We use the term, but really, what is it? Simply put, it's *the mutual sharing of life between two people*.

For a relationship to exist there has to be "mutualability." Each person has to make some contribution for the relationship to exist. Both need to participate in some way or it won't work.

≈ Sharing life means being genuine with each other. It's standing in front of a person and saying, "This is who I am!" No disclaimers or apologies. ≈

You may say you have a wonderful relationship with Billy Graham. You've read all of his books, attended many of his crusades, heard him speak at prayer breakfasts, contributed to his ministry and pray for him daily. But if you're unknown to him, you really don't have a relationship.

For a relationship to be maintained and grow, each participant must contribute. If a relationship fails, each one has made some contribution to that aspect as well (even though each may not bear equal responsibility for the failure).

The Need for Sincerity

Do you know what sharing life means? It means being genuine with each other. This is the quality of being who you really are without a front or a façade. It's standing in front of a person and saying, "This is who I am!" No disclaimers or apologies, either.

A main ingredient in genuineness is sincerity. When each person is sincere, you can relax in the comfort and security that he or she is trustworthy. The word sincere comes from a Latin word which means "without wax." In ancient times, fine expensive porcelain often developed tiny cracks when it was fired in the kiln. The dishonest merchants would smear pearly white wax over the cracks until they disappeared, then claim the porcelain was unblemished. But when the porcelain was held up to the sun, the light would reveal the cracks filled in with wax. So honest merchants marked their porcelain with the word "sin-cere"—without wax. That's what is meant by genuine sincerity: no hidden cracks, no ulterior motives, no hidden agendas.[3] Are you a person of sincerity? What about the person you're interested in?

You just can't build a relationship with someone who isn't sincere and transparent.

Who do you have in your life like this at the present time? Who have you had in your life like this?[4]

Levels of Relationships

As we move through life interacting with others, we don't experience the same depth of relationship with everyone we know. There are several different levels of relationships. For example, you don't have the same kind of relationship with acquaintances at work that you have with your immediate family.

Sometimes the intensity of a relationship is the result of planned activity on our part. For instance, you may purposely cultivate a friendship with a new person at church to make him feel included.

But sometimes relationships just happen—such as being drawn to someone who enjoys the same hobby you enjoy. Many factors determine the different levels of relationship we experience with the people in our lives.

Casual and Binding Relationships
One way to look at relational levels is to see them either as *casual* or *binding*. Binding relationships may include those with spouse, parents, children, in-laws and other relatives, bosses and coworkers, or any relationship which is valued as permanent or

long-term. Of course, it may not be highly valued. We may be stuck with it.

Casual relationships are those you share with neighbors, distant friends, acquaintances or anyone you relate to apart from a permanent or long-term commitment. Obligations to binding relationships are—or should be—greater than is the case with casual relationships. Since binding relationships are permanent, there are very few valid reasons for terminating them. However, you may find yourself in a binding relationship, such as with a relative or even in a dating relationship, which is being treated by one or both parties as a casual relationship. A lack of commitment when it is expected can put a strain on your relationship and cause tension between the two of you. Clarifying expectations, especially in binding relationships, is essential to getting along with those closest to you.[5]

There will be some casual relationships in your life that you honestly wish didn't exist. We've all had coworkers or even people at church who were unpleasant to be around or with whom we just didn't "click."

And we all have one or more binding relationships that we wish were merely casual relationships! We would have no reason to interact with some of our relatives if a family connection didn't exist through blood or marriage. True? We just don't have much in common. But uncomfortable relationships like these need not be irritating or burdensome. We can learn to get along with these people through the presence of Jesus Christ, who can change our attitudes.

Minimal Relationships

Another way to look at varying levels of relationships is to think of them as *minimal, moderate, strong* or *quality*. Consider the differences.

Minimal relationships involve simple, surface-level verbal interaction which is generally pleasant instead of hostile. People at this level usually do not give or receive help, emotional support or love from each other. They just speak and listen to each other when necessary. You may have someone like this in your life for several years and, suddenly, the relationship develops into a romance.

You will cultivate a minimal relationship with the people you are uncomfortable around, but with whom you must relate to some degree. The key to getting along is to determine in advance how much you are required to interact with them and then strive to make that interaction as healthy as possible. It will take some effort and patience on your part.

Who are the people in your life today that fit the classification of minimal relationships? What are your feelings about them at this time? Have you ever had a long-term dating relationship that was stuck here?

Moderate Relationships

A moderate relationship has all the characteristics of a minimal relationship, but includes one more: an emotional attachment. Now you're getting somewhere! In moderate relationships, you want emotional support and you're willing to give it. There is an openness which enables both of you to listen to the other's hurts, concerns, joys and needs. Ideally, this openness is a two-way street. It's a good beginning. But even when it's not, we believers are called to respond with openness regardless of the other person's response.

Emotional support is the foundation upon which deep relationships can be built. For example, a marriage that is not based on an emotional bond between partners will not be a fulfilling marriage. You've seen them. So have I. They're married singles living under the same roof!

Often we become the instigator for moderate relationships by taking the first steps of emotional openness and support. Others may follow suit, or they could be threatened by our move. It may be hard for them to trust you with their pent-up emotions. They could be living with leftover hurts. Then all you can do is take the risk to be open and reach out. It's all right for people to move slowly toward emotional openness. Moderate relationships take time to build.

Who are the people in your life today who fit the classification of moderate relationships? What are your feelings about them? If you're in a dating relationship now, is it at this level? For you or for both?

Strong Relationships

The difference between a moderate relationship and a strong one is found in one simple word—*help*. Strong relationships develop when you have high involvement with people. You do this by reaching out to minister to them in tangible ways. You're ready to provide help when they need it. You also accept help from them when you need it.

For some, the helping aspect is easier than the emotional aspect. In fact, I've seen many bypass the emotional attachment and go straight to helping. The personal investment is less. And yet, strong relationships *must* be based on emotional support for caring to be meaningful. Short-circuiting emotional support leads to shallow relationships. Emotional support is a stronger tie than helping.

Who are the people in your life today with whom you share strong relationships? What are your feelings about them at this time? If you're in a dating relationship, is it at this level yet?

Quality Relationships

All the elements of the previous levels lead to the deepest level of all: quality relationships. This includes the added element of loving trust. You feel safe with this person when you reveal what's going on inside you—your inner needs, thoughts and feelings. He treats what you share as a gift. You also feel free to invite him to share his inner needs, thoughts and feelings—and he feels safe in doing so.

Quality relationships can exist between friends, spouses, parents, children and even coworkers. There are no secrets and no barriers. The relationship is built upon complete mutual trust.

What people in your life today come under the heading of quality relationships? How do you feel about them at this time?[6] If you're dating someone, are you here yet?

Keep in mind that the way you approach a relationship can make it or break it. The first few months of a relationship or a marriage need to be nurtured like an infant taking baby steps and just learning to walk and talk, rather than treated as an adult. Too often, two people perceive their relationship too soon as a fully

≈ Think of yourself as a battery. Depleting relationships drain you. It's difficult to have enough juice left to even get started again! ≈

developed, mature adult and their expectations are soon dissolved. But if you see it as an infant, for that's what it is, you'll adjust your expectations accordingly.

Relational Energy Levels

There's one other factor to be considered when examining a relationship, no matter at what level the relationship exists. A relationship is going to be either a *depleting* or a *replenishing* one. A depleting relationship is one in which you are with someone who drains you emotionally and spiritually. It taps into your energy reserves in some way. It can happen in long-term dating relationships or in a marriage. Being around this type of person is just plain hard work. At first the relationship may seem workable, but soon it becomes an exercise in depletion and coping. It's not a pretty picture.

Those who deplete you contribute to your problems rather than help you resolve them. If you think of yourself as a battery, these are the people who drain you. It's difficult to have enough juice left to even get started again!

You don't want a depleting relationship—in any kind of a situation. You want replenishment—relationships with people who energize and vitalize you just by being with them. They add to your life in a positive way. And one of the best ways to draw people like this is to be that kind of person yourself.[7]

Finding Someone to Love

In her book, *How to Stop Looking for Someone Perfect and Find Someone to Love*, Judith Sills suggests three rules to keep in mind when looking for a lifelong partner. These rules are presented to give you something to think about when you find yourself swamped by your emotions. Dr. Sills says:

> It's easy to get swamped with feelings when you are in the process of mating. God knows, sexual arousal alone can make the brightest among us absolute sapheads. Mix in a little loneliness, a fair share of hope, a history of disappointment, and a healthy dose of social pressure and you've got all the ingredients for the emotional morass that so often accompanies courtship.[8]

1. The Availability Element

The first rule is so basic it's almost redundant to mention it. *Is the person available for marriage?* Attraction doesn't always wait to check this out. When you're looking for a lifelong partner, why waste time on those who "may be available in the future"? After all, no one picks out a horse to bet on that isn't even in the race![9]

Among those you should consider to be unavailable are:

People who are in their 30s and still living with their parents. If they have never lived on their own, or have never emotionally separated from their parents, or are not emotionally capable of living 3,000 miles from their parents, they don't meet the criteria of those who have the best prospects for a lasting marriage. Thus, you don't have a candidate.

People who are separated from their spouses or involved in dating someone else. Those who are separated are still legally married in the eyes of the state and of God, even if they say, "Well, we really haven't been a married couple for the last two years." They're still married!

Remember, anyone who divorces needs to complete a divorce recovery program at least once (many repeat the process) and needs at least a year of no involvement for the healing process to occur. The longer they wait, the greater the possibility of the next marriage succeeding.

If you're considering getting involved with someone who is divorced, aside from the recovery time, keep in mind two other issues: children and the person's financial obligations now that they're divorced. If there are children, you are marrying a family, not just a person.

Perhaps one or both of you have been married before. It's vital to assess this current relationship carefully if you are considering marriage. It's amazing how many divorced people later marry someone who is similar to their first spouse, or someone to whom they respond in the same unproductive way. To avoid repeating your previous experience, it may be helpful for you and your intended to complete the "Preparing for the Next Marriage" form in appendix I.

A person who is currently in a relationship with someone else is also unavailable. This person needs to experience closure from this current involvement as well as a time of recovery instead of overlapping the two relationships. Those who have a pattern of overlapping are risk-avoiders. They don't want to be alone so they hang on until another possibility comes along. When they're sure the new one might work, then they make the break. Keep in mind that if they did this to one person, you could be the next on the list.

Finally, a person who isn't interested in a long-term relationship or isn't ready emotionally is not a candidate. If the individual has previously experienced long-term relationships rather than a pattern of two-month involvements, there may be more hope.

2. What You See Is What You Get

The second rule that Dr. Sills proposes is: *There are no substitutions.* What you see is what you get. Perhaps you've seen signs in restaurants that say *No Substitutions.* This means that if you ordered a meal, you take whatever is on the plate. If what accompanies the filet mignon is broccoli and cauliflower, you don't have a choice. It's yours!

The person you marry may not—no, *will* not—fulfill your wish list of everything you want in a mate. You need to discover what qualities your candidate lacks as soon as possible and

≈ The person you marry will NOT fulfill your wish list of everything you want in a mate. Discover what qualities your candidate lacks as soon as possible and determine whether you can live without these for the rest of your life. ≈

determine whether you can live without these for the rest of your life. If you don't discover them beforehand, you *will* later and your response will probably be stronger. In fact, the rule is, the sooner discoveries are made the easier it is for you to adjust. But the longer it takes, the more upset you are. Why? Because you feel betrayed! You're angry at the other person for not letting you know, and angry at yourself for not discovering the problem in the first place.

Remember that all candidates come with psychological, emotional, physical and spiritual flaws. The older they are, the more history (a polite term for baggage) they bring. Everyone comes this way—yes, even you. And we all share another feature in common. We're all sinners! The grace that God extends to us helps us extend grace to others as well.

I'm sure you have already made a mental list defining who could be a candidate for you and who couldn't. But once again, instead of talking about it, put it in writing. And instead of making a dream list of those you want, make a list of those you *wouldn't want.* Complete this statement:

I wouldn't consider anyone as a partner who...

1. _isn't a Christian (growing)_
2. _drinks heavily_
3. _smokes a "does" drugs_
4. _has an explosive/time bomb temper_
5. _____

Now, what does this tell you about yourself? Why did these factors end up on your list? Why are they so undesirable? A screening process like this can save you both time and heartache.

3. Your Mirror Image
The third guideline is, *How does this person make you feel about yourself?* Have you ever considered how important a mate's opinion of you becomes? You will be influenced by how the other person perceives you. As you look at your partner, it's as though you are seeing who you are in a mirror. What if your partner is highly critical of you or has unreasonable expectations? What if he constantly gives you messages that leave you feeling helpless, non-functional, guilty, valueless or depressed?

I remember a couple from more than 20 years ago who were engaged to be married. She appeared somewhat submissive and compliant, but he was strong, overbearing, dominant and critical. In other words he was quite obnoxious. After several sessions of premarital counseling, they stopped for a while. Three months later the young woman broke up with him because of his behavior and attitude.

During the engagement this woman had been stressed and quite depressed. But several months later I ran into her at a social gathering and had to look twice. She appeared so much more attractive and radiant. The physical effects of stress and depression had disappeared. Why? Because the mirror image she had been staring at for two years was no longer in the picture. His influence was gone, and she had the opportunity to see herself as she really was.

What about your partner? Does his or her view of you build you up? Does her presence and attitude help you feel valued or worthless? Does your partner enhance your strengths and bring out your potential? Does he help you blossom and be more than you could be by yourself? Are you freer to love, to grow, to really reflect who you are?

A friend shared a story with me about his own experience with his wife. Perhaps you're aware of the story he refers to—the one about Johnny Lingo. It's the best example I've heard to describe how a partner can affect his mate in a positive way.

> When I married my wife, we both were insecure and she did everything she could to try to please me. I didn't realize how dominating and uncaring I was toward her. My actions in our early marriage caused her to withdraw even more. I wanted her to wear her hair long and be perfect at all times. I wanted her to be feminine and sensual.
>
> The more I wanted her to change, the more withdrawn and insecure she felt. I was causing her to be the opposite of what I wanted her to be. I began to realize the demands I was putting on her, not so much by words but by body language.
>
> By God's grace I learned that I must love the woman I married, not the woman of my fantasies. I made a commitment to love Susan for who she was—who God created her to be.
>
> The change came about in a very interesting way. During a trip to Atlanta I read an article in *Reader's Digest*. I made a copy of it, and I have kept it in my heart and mind ever since.
>
> It was the story of Johnny Lingo, a man who lived in the South Pacific. The islanders all spoke highly of this man, but when it came time for him to find a wife the people shook their heads in disbelief. In order to obtain a wife you paid for her by giving her father cows. Four to

six cows was considered a high price. But the woman Johnny Lingo chose was plain, skinny and walked with her shoulders hunched and her head down. She was very hesitant and shy. What surprised everyone was Johnny's offer—he gave eight cows for her! Everyone chuckled about it, since they believed his father-in-law had put one over on him.

Several months after the wedding, a visitor from the U.S. came to the islands to trade and heard the story about Johnny Lingo and his eight-cow wife. Upon meeting Johnny and his wife, the visitor was completely taken aback. This wasn't a shy, plain, hesitant woman, but one who was beautiful, poised and confident. The visitor asked about the transformation, and Johnny Lingo's response was very simple. "I wanted an eight-cow woman," he said, "and when I paid that for her and treated her in that fashion, she began to believe that she was an eight-cow woman. She discovered she was worth more than any other woman in the islands. And what matters most is what a woman thinks about herself."

This simple story impacted my life. I immediately sent Susan flowers. (I had rarely, if ever, done that before.) The message on the card simply said, "To My Eight-Cow Wife." The florist, who was a friend of mine, thought I had lost my mind and questioned if that was really what I wanted to say.

Susan received the flowers with total surprise and bewilderment at the card. When I returned from the trip, I told her that I loved her for who she is and that I considered her to be my eight-cow wife, and then I gave her the article to read.

I now look for ways to show her I am proud of her and how much I appreciate her. An example of this involved a ring. When we became engaged I gave Susan an antique engagement ring that I inherited from a great-great aunt. Susan seemed very pleased, and I never thought any more about it. But I had come out cheap, and that's how she felt. After 20 years of marriage she shared with me how she felt about the hand-me-down wedding ring. We had our whole family get involved in learning about diamonds. Susan found one she liked. It was not the largest stone nor the most expensive. I would have gladly paid more. I bought it and gave it to her for Christmas. "To My Eight-Cow Wife, With All My Love!" But what this did for our relationship is amazing.

First, it changed me! My desire began to change. My desire now is for Susan to be all that God has designed her to be. It is my responsibility as her husband to allow her that freedom.

It also changed her. Susan became free. She learned who she is in Christ. She has gained confidence and self-assurance.

How will these three rules assist you as you evaluate your current partner or someone in the future?[10] Consider the partners you've had in the past. How did your relationship with them...

1. Make you feel about yourself?

2. Increase your feelings of value about yourself?

3. Encourage you to take positive steps you never would have taken?

4. Make your life more significant than it was before?

You've been thinking of potential partners, someone you could perhaps spend the rest of your life with. But what kind of partner will *you* be? It's important that you complete the following exercise since you, too, are someone's potential partner.

Why would someone want to spend the rest of his or her life with me?

1. I'm a growing Christian
2. I'm sensitive (esp. to the Holy Spirit)
3. I'm beautiful
4. I desire to be married + have children
5. I'm good with children
6. I'm intelligent + have a decent education
7. I have a career + goals
8. I am organized + generally efficient
9. I've overcome a great deal
10. I'm fun to be around
    I'm creative (would be in a relationship)
    I value relationships

*Why **wouldn't** a person want to spend the rest of his or her life with me?*

1. I'm overweight
2. I have a great deal of debt
3. Even though I've overcome a lot — I have baggage
4. I'm sensitive (sometimes overly)
5. I cry a lot / have some good mood swings
6. I'm sassy + smart-aleck sometimes
7. I can clerk too much (foot in mouth)
8.
9.
10.

Notes

1. Robbie Castleman, *True Love in a World of False Hope* (Downers Grove, Ill.: InterVarsity Press, 1966), pp. 148-150. Adapted.
2. Max Lucado, *On the Anvil* (Wheaton, Ill.: Tyndale House Publishers, 1985), pp. 69, 70.
3. Charles Swindoll, *The Quest for Character* (Sisters, Oreg.: Multnomah Books, 1988), p. 67. Adapted.
4. Tom Marshall, *Right Relationships: How to Create Them and How to Restore Them* (Kent, England: Sovereign World, 1992), pp. 10-14. Adapted.
5. Myron Rush, *Hope for Hurting Relationships* (Wheaton, Ill.: Victor Books, 1989), p. 29. Adapted.
6. Carol C. Flax and Earl Ubell, *Mother, Father, You* (Ridgefield, Conn.: Wyden Books, 1980), pp. 192-201. Adapted.
7. Ronnie W. Floyd, *Choices* (Nashville: Broadman & Holman, 1994), pp. 170-174. Adapted.
8. Dr. Judith Sills, *How to Stop Looking for Someone Perfect and Find Someone to Love* (New York: Ballantine Books, 1984), pp. 34, 35.
9. Op. cit., p. 36. Adapted.
10. Op. cit., pp. 33-55. Adapted.

The Four Pillars
of a Relationship

≈

The basics of a relationship are like the pillars
or foundation stones of a house. All must be strong.
If you try to make up for one weak pillar by
strengthening another, the whole structure
will be out of balance.

If someone were to ask you the question, "What are the factors necessary for a lasting relationship?" what would you say? What foundation stones or "pillars" are essential for strong relationships?

Think about it. What if you had to limit them to just four factors? There are actually many, but what is needed in any relationship, especially a lifelong marriage, are the following: *love, trust, respect* and *understanding.*

The most *lasting* of these is *love.* Paul indicated this when he said that faith, hope and love "abide" or remain, but that "the greatest of these is love" (1 Cor. 13:13). He also said:

Therefore, as God's chosen people, holy and dearly loved,

clothe yourselves with compassion, kindness, humility, gentleness and patience. Bear with each other and forgive whatever grievances you may have against one another. Forgive as the Lord forgave you (Col. 3:12,13).

The most *fragile* of these four pillars is *trust*. The most *neglected* one is *respect* or honor. The one that takes the *longest* to develop is *understanding* or knowledge.

These are like four pillars of a house. Each of these pillars must be nurtured. If one is weak you can't make up for the lack in that area by adding to another. Love won't make up for mistrust, nor understanding for disrespect. Look at what happens.

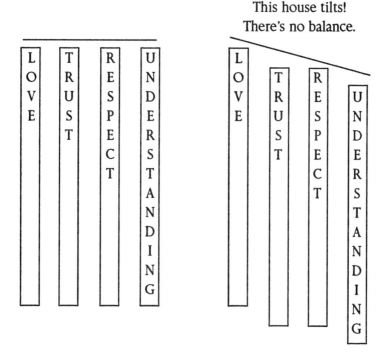

This house tilts!
There's no balance.

The Pillar of Love

By now you've probably heard multiple messages about the different types of biblical love—*eros, philia, storge* and *agape*. But how are such loves expressed in practical and enduring ways?[1] There are several characteristics.

Safety and Security

You want to feel safe and secure in your relationship. You want to be able to breathe a sigh of relief and say, "It's nice to relax with someone, let down the protective armor and be myself." This is the characteristic we enjoy so much in friendship-love (*philia*). And if this dimension of love is present in a marriage, it's an indication that there's hope for the relationship.

In which of your relationships do you feel most safe and secure? Who are the people who best convey this characteristic? What do they do that communicates safety and security to you?

Support

People want and need to feel supported by those who care for them. This is mentioned in another chapter, but it needs to be expanded here.

A supportive relationship helps you know you're not facing the world alone. You can depend on others to stand with you in difficult times, even when they don't necessarily agree with your stand. Do you have some supportive persons in your life? Who are they? Do they include the person you're interested in as a possible spouse?

A supportive person is not only needed during difficult times, but also during good times. When you support others, you encourage them, help them dream and grow, even to the point that they exceed your own level of growth or ability. You use your strengths, capabilities and skills to lift the other person above yourself. This is sometimes particularly hard for men. Can you handle this?

Occasionally I meet former students of mine from Talbot Seminary and discover that they've excelled in some areas of their lives beyond my own level of ability or achievement. That's wonderful! I have a "Yes!" response.

Also, being an avid fisherman, I receive tremendous satisfaction helping others enjoy fishing by learning the skills that will help them haul in the big ones. (Yes, there's more to fishing than luck!) And if they catch more fish than I do as a result of the support I give them, all the better! We rejoice together. I've seen my wife and daughter outfish me.

The key to support is discovering the strengths of others and building on those qualities to help them succeed. To do this, you need a positive attitude toward them. You've got to look for the best in them. You must believe in them until they believe in themselves and start succeeding.

It happens all the time in my counseling office. I see shattered families and individuals; they are broken, troubled, and hurting. Often I need to lend them my hope and faith until they can generate some of their own. I must support them by believing in them, their strengths and their future until they are stable enough to believe for themselves.

This is an important way for your love to be reflected in a relationship. There will be times when you need support, and times when you need to give it.

If you are currently in a relationship, in what way do each of you support the other?

Sense of Belonging

Every one of us knows the pain of being excluded or rejected. We all have a built-in, God-given need for a sense of belonging that comes from being included by others. It makes you feel significant because someone else has opened his or her own private world to you. It's easy to get along with those who accept you, open their hearts to you and include you in their lives.

The older I get, the more value I place on the sense of belonging I enjoy with my wife and a few close friends. I can share my hurts, my dreams, my thoughts and my feelings with these people without fear of being put down, laughed at or rejected. It feels so comfortable to belong. Having received the benefits of belonging, I want to help others feel included.

Who do you have in your life who communicates to you a sense of belonging like this?

Care

We all need somebody to care about us and nurture us. When you nurture someone, you invite him or her to take a special place in your heart. You express your care through words as well as through your deeds. When you really care about someone, you are willing to move out of your comfort zone for that person's benefit. It's almost impossible not to connect with someone who cares enough about you to make such a move.

Expressing genuine care may not be convenient. You may be called on to...

- Go shopping for several hours.
- Sleep out in a tent on the hard ground.
- Travel for several hours just to eat at a "unique" restaurant.
- Listen to the other person well beyond your usual attention span.

But because you care for the other person, you're willing to extend yourself in these ways—with a positive attitude! And you would be reflecting *agape* love, the sacrificial love that is at the heart of Scripture.

Acceptance

I want to be accepted by others. So do you. When we accept others for who they are, we free them from the pressure of being molded into the persons we want them to be. When you accept others, you become compatible with them and get along with them.

How does the "significant other" in your life show he or she accepts you?[2]

The Pillar of Trust

When it comes to trust, a sign should be hung over it saying, "Handle with Care." Some people find it easy to trust, while others find it very difficult.

Trust is making yourself dependent upon another person for some result or outcome. It's a healthy dependency. You can't be forced into it. It's a voluntary response. It's an attitude, and it has three parts.

First, you *believe* in your mind that the other person is trustworthy. Can you list several people in your life at the present time whom you believe to be trustworthy? Why do you believe this?

≈ Relationships require trust. But there is a risk in trust. The other person could let you down. All life involves some risk, but loving makes you especially vulnerable. ≈

Second, there is an *emotional response* in trust. You feel assurance or confidence in trusting the other person. Who comes to mind here?

Finally, your *behavior* has to come into play when you *act* on the trust you perceive.

Trust is when you're in the water and a friend reaches down his hand to pull you out and you reach up and grasp it. You don't hesitate or debate whether he really wants to rescue you. You believe. You feel confident. You reach out.

But there is a risk in trust. The other person could let you down. Although all life involves some risk, loving makes you especially vulnerable. In fact, you can't be in a loving relationship unless you're willing to run the risk of being hurt. How do you know if you really trust the other person or not? You don't have a backup plan in case the other person lets you down. You don't have a plan "B" in case he or she fails you.

I've seen the subtle ways trust is undermined in marriages. For example, a person says he will do something but his partner calls him or leaves reminder notes to be sure he does it, or even calls a store to check on him.

Yes, it's true. When you trust, you're vulnerable.

When two people in a relationship have mutual trust, they are sending messages to one another.

They are saying, "I have confidence in you."

They are saying, "I will be here for you when no one else is."

They are saying, "You can depend on me for little and large things."

They are saying, "I will be consistent, not changeable or impulsive."

They are saying, "You can depend on me to speak the truth."

So the question is this: If you are in a relationship, to what degree is that person trustworthy?

And yes, the next question is, *Are you a person of trust?*

The Pillar of Respect

A third foundation for a relationship—respect or honor—is the most neglected.

Throughout Scripture we are told to honor one another. Have you been honored or respected by others? If so, you know what this concept means. It *must* occur between partners in a significant relationship.

Basically, respect is recognizing and acknowledging the other person's worth or value. Significantly, this requires that you honor and respect yourself; for if you don't respect yourself how can you give respect to someone else?[3]

Do you understand the extent of your own value and worth? It's nothing you earn; it's been given to you by God.

Let's remember how God sees us. He doesn't compare you with the other people He has created. He has given you your own capabilities and potential. He expects you to develop and use only what He has given you, not what He has given someone else. He wants you to develop and use what you have so you won't miss out on life. You are God's workmanship:

For we are His workmanship, created in Christ Jesus for

good works, which God prepared beforehand, that we
should walk in them (Eph. 2:10, *NASB*).

Jesus Christ invites us to come to Him by faith, believing that
He will accept us as we are into His family:

> But as many as received Him, to them He gave the right to
> become children of God, even to those who believe in His
> name, who were born not of blood, nor of the will of the
> flesh, nor of the will of man, but of God (John 1:12,13, *NASB*).

> Therefore having been justified by faith, we have peace
> with God through our Lord Jesus Christ (Rom. 5:1, *NASB*).

If God and Jesus Christ are with us at all times, we need not
feel inferior or inadequate. God is our source of adequacy. We
can love ourselves without pangs of guilt. We can love ourselves
without having to defend our actions.

Dr. Lloyd Ahlem, in *Do I Have to Be Me?*, summarizes what
God has done for us.

> The writers of the Scriptures are careful to point out that
> when God looks at you in Jesus Christ, He sees you as a
> brother to His own Son....You are worth all of God's atten-
> tion. If you were the only person in the world, it would be
> worth God's effort to make Himself known to you and to
> love you. He gives you freely the status and adequacy of an
> heir to the universe.[4]

A few years ago, the choir at our church sang an anthem based
on Zephaniah 3:17. I had never heard the song before. The words
were printed in our church bulletin, and I have read them many
times since because they encourage me, inspire me and remind
me of what I mean to God:

> And the Father will dance over you in joy!

He will take delight in whom He loves.
Is that a choir I hear singing the praises of God?
No, the Lord God Himself is exulting over you in song!
And He will joy over you in song!
My soul will make its boast in God,
For He has answered all my cries.
His faithfulness to me is as sure as the dawn of a new day.
Awake my soul, and sing!
Let my spirit rejoice in God!
Sing, O daughter of Zion, with all of your heart!
Cast away fear for you have been restored!
Put on the garment of praise as on a festival day.
Join with the Father in glorious, jubilant song.
God rejoices over you in song![5]

In his fascinating book, *The Pleasures of God*, John Piper beautifully expresses how God desires to do good to all who hope in Him. Dr. Piper writes about God singing, and asks:

What do you hear when you imagine the voice of God singing? I hear the booming of Niagara Falls mingled with the trickle of a mossy mountain stream. I hear the blast of Mt. St. Helen's mingled with a kitten's purr. I hear the power of an East Coast hurricane and the barely audible puff of a night snow in the woods. And I hear the unimaginable roar of the sun, 865,000 miles thick, 1,300,000 times bigger than the earth, and nothing but fire, 1,000,000 degrees centigrade on the cooler surface of the corona. But I hear this unimaginable roar mingled with the tender, warm crackling of logs in the living room on a cozy winter's night.

I stand dumbfounded, staggered, speechless that he is singing over me—one who has dishonored him so many times and in so many ways. It is almost too good to be true. He is rejoicing over my good with all his heart and all his soul. He virtually breaks forth into song when he hits upon a new way to do me good.[6]

Did you catch the significance of how God feels about you and what He wants for you? If you would remind yourself of this each morning, how would that impact your day?

You have value. But so does the person you're interested in. The higher the value of something, the greater the care and attention we pay to it. A $1,000 diamond does not have the same level of protection and security as a $10-million-dollar gem. Your value? And everyone else's? Simply this: "For God so loved the world that he gave his one and only Son, that whoever believes in him shall not perish but have eternal life" (John 3:16).

How to Show Respect

How do we honor and respect another person? There are several simple steps:

You show *acceptance.* This is an attitude that welcomes a person with regard. It's saying to your partner in word and deed,

> ≈ Showing respect means you give affirmation and encouragement. You're a cheerleader, believing in others even when they don't believe in themselves. ≈

"I'm glad you're a part of my life." Think of an example of how you do this. Think of how the other person in your life does this for you.

You give *recognition.* This shows that you are observant as to who others are and what they are doing. Your response to them is not disinterest, or mere toleration. Think of an example of how you do give recognition, and of how the other person in your life does this for you.

You give *affirmation and encouragement.* You believe in others, and you look for ways to build them up. You're a cheerleader, believing in them even when they don't believe in themselves. You don't take for granted what they do or who they are. Paul counsels, "Therefore encourage one another and build each other up, just as in fact you are doing" (1 Thess. 5:11). Think of an example of how you do this, and of how the other person in your life does this for you.

You give *appreciation*. This is something quite personal. You're expressing your pleasure in being a part of this person's life. Give an example of how you do this, and of how the other person in your life does this for you.

You give *admiration*. This is giving credit to such an extent that you're saying, "I wish I had your ability." Give an example of how you and your significant other do this for each other.

All these ways of showing respect are communicated by what you say and what you don't say to each other, as well as by your nonverbal communication and by just being there for that person.[7]

The Pillar of Understanding

The fourth essential element of a close relationship—and the one that is so often short-circuited—is understanding.

The first three elements are dependent upon this one. Understanding only develops over time. It's based on knowledge. You understand others by getting inside of them and seeing life from their perspective, through their eyes. It involves a tremendous amount of communication—of asking, sharing and listening.

Your partner will never understand you unless you reveal yourself. Nor will you ever understand another unless he or she is open with you. What is revealed is based on trust, which is based on how well you know one another, which is based on what is revealed.[8]

The Risk of Relationship

All these pillars or foundation stones of close relationships involve an ingredient called *risk*. Neither love, nor trust, nor respect, nor understanding will lead to a loving relationship unless both partners are willing to risk being vulnerable.

So everything boils down to being willing to risk. This is the foundation and the basis of all relationships. Through this you can discover who is best for you and who isn't—always keeping in mind the spiritual dimension.

Since relationships are risky, the choice to have a meaningful, lasting connection with a significant other may not be an easy choice. However, the rewards of an intimate relationship make it one of the greatest choices you will ever make.

Notes

1. Tom Marshall, *Right Relationships: How to Create Them and How to Restore Them* (Kent, England: Sovereign World, 1992), p. 29. Adapted.
2. H. Norman Wright, *How to Get Along with Almost Anyone* (Dallas, Tex.: Word Publishing, 1989), pp. 54-58. Adapted.
3. Marshall, op. cit., pp. 44-60. Adapted.
4. Lloyd Ahlem, *Do I Have to Be Me?* (Ventura, Calif.: Regal Books, 1973), pp. 46-47.
5. "And the Father Will Dance." Arranged by Mark Hayes.
6. John Piper, *The Pleasures of God* (Sisters, Oreg.: Multnomah Books, 1991), p. 188.
7. Marshall, op. cit., pp. 62-73. Adapted.
8. Ibid., pp. 86-90. Adapted.

Where Did YOU Come From?

≈

*The atmosphere in your family of origin,
and especially your relationship with your parents,
will significantly impact your relationships
and shape your identity and behavior.*

"Where did you come from?" and "What are you bringing with you?"

Strange questions? Sure. But your answers to these questions are essential—if you want a relationship that's going to work. When you enter a relationship, you bring something to it called *baggage*. It can help you get around or get in your way. That's why you need to look at the home background that you and your significant other bring to a relationship, and how it will affect the way you respond to one another. Pay special attention to the bulleted and italicized questions that follow the following descriptions of some of the baggage people often bring into a relationship.

First, let's consider two individuals. Each is in a serious relationship with another person.

Kay

Kay is a 20-year-old junior attending a college 2,000 miles from home. She is planning to be married in eight months. "Dad calls me every other day to get advice or to complain about Mother," she told me. "He tells me things he should have shared with Mother over the years. I've probably received more attention from him than from my mother or any of the other kids. I thought that when I went away to school, I wouldn't have to be this involved with my family. But it hasn't changed. Why has this happened? And how is it going to affect my marriage? Will he do this after I'm married?"

- *What is Kay saying about her family of origin? How will this affect her relationship?*

Mary

Mary is a perfectionist. Her dress is impeccable, and everything about her is precise. It's difficult for her to relax because she feels that she is always on display. Her fiancé is more laid back and accepting. He keeps encouraging her not to be so structured and uptight.

Mary told me that her parents were divorced when she was four. When her mother remarried several years later, Mary found out that her stepfather saw her as a "necessary nuisance"—that's what he called her. He was a cold, rigid workaholic.

"Do you know why I'm such a perfectionist?" Mary asked me. "It's true there are some benefits to perfectionism, but at times I wonder if there isn't a better way to live."

- *What factors in Mary's home may have contributed to her perfectionism? How might these affect her marriage?*

The Functional Family

It's good that Kay and Mary are asking these questions before their relationships go any further.

Many factors combine to make us who we are. You're the product of your family birth order, neurological structure and interactions with your mother, father, siblings, and so on. But the atmosphere of your childhood home, and especially your relationship with your parents, will have a significant impact on shaping your identity and behavior as well as impacting your relationships.

If you were reared in a healthy home, you're fortunate. These families are called functional or healthy families because they function effectively and productively.

Functional families display many of the following positive qualities. Rate each of these on a scale of 0 to 10 to help you discover what you're bringing with you to a relationship.

1. The climate of the home was positive. The atmosphere was basically nonjudgmental.   0_____10
2. Each member of the family was valued and accepted for who he or she was. There was regard for individual characteristics.   0_____10
3. Each person was allowed to operate within his or her proper role. A child was allowed to be a child and an adult was an adult.   0_____10
4. Members of the family cared for one another, and verbalized their caring and affirmation.   0_____10
5. The communication process was healthy, open, and direct, with no double messages.   0_____10
6. Children were reared in such a way that they could mature and become individuals in their own right. They separated from Mom and Dad in a healthy manner.   0_____10
7. The family enjoyed being together. They did not get together merely out of a sense of obligation, nor do they now.   0_____10

8. Family members could laugh together, and they still enjoy life together. 0____10
9. Family members could share their hopes, dreams, fears, and concerns with one another and still be accepted. A healthy level of intimacy existed within the home. 0____10

These are qualities we would all like to have in our families when we marry.

- *To what degree do you see your family of origin as healthy?*

The Dysfunctional Family

The characteristics of a healthy, functional family are just the opposite of those of what we call a dysfunctional family. Dysfunctional families lack much of the acceptance, openness, affirmation, communication, love and togetherness of a healthy family.

Families That Are Off Course

Several times a year I travel on airplanes. So far I've always arrived at my intended destination, mainly because the plane stayed on course. If my plane were to stray off course just a few degrees, I might end up in Cuba instead of Washington, D.C. The longer a plane travels off course, the farther it wanders from its destination.

A dysfunctional family is one that has strayed off course. Though they probably don't think of it in these terms, every newly married couple wants to build a functional family. Their "destination" is a loving, healthy, happy relationship between husband and wife, parents and children. But many little things can go wrong in families: Feelings get hurt, needs and expectations go unmet. If these minor midcourse errors are not corrected, greater problems arise: Love and acceptance are withheld, "me" and "mine" take priority over "us" and "ours." Soon the prospective "happy family" is far off course and exhibiting many other troubling characteristics.

- *Describe ways your family was "on course."*
- *In what ways was it off course?*
- *Describe how your partner's family was "on course."*
- *How was your partner's family dysfunctional?*

Many children from dysfunctional families are thrust into adulthood feeling empty and incomplete, afraid and unable to trust because their needs went unmet. And when they don't feel secure in themselves, they look for some type of security outside themselves. They're always trying to fill up the empty space inside.

This quest to have needs met leads a person to do one or all of three things: (1) create or adopt compulsive or addictive behavior patterns; (2) make a poor choice of marital partner; (3) place impossible demands upon his or her spouse after marriage.

Any family can become dysfunctional for a period of time. Sometimes during a crisis, Mom, Dad, and the kids don't function at their normal levels. Often someone else—such as a pastor or a counselor—has to step in and help them survive until they get back to normal. But in a truly dysfunctional family the crisis is perpetual and the roles of the family members are usually constant.

One of the best descriptions of this kind of family comes from author Sara Hines Martin:

It can be a home where a parent or grandparent is chronically ill or mentally ill, or a home where a parent is emotionally ill, including chronically depressed. It could also be a home where one parent dies and the surviving parent is so overcome by grief, he or she is unable to cope with the parenting tasks; a home where physical and/or sexual abuse takes place; a home where suicide has taken place; a home where a child was adopted; and the rigidly religious home. (This last category surprises many people because nothing is specifically done, as in the other categories. This type of home produces similar dynamics because children are not valued for themselves but are raised by rigid rules. The father, if a minister, may neglect his family while carrying out his work. The children can get the feeling they must make the parents look good in the eyes of the community.) In summary, these families focus on a problem, addiction, trauma or some "secret" rather than on the child. The home is shame-and-blame-based.[1]

The phrase "shame-and-blame" is one of the best descriptions for this type of home. It is totally contrary to the pattern of love and acceptance presented in the Scriptures.

Families that stray off course display several telltale traits. How many of these exist in a family and how often they occur reflect how far the family has strayed from healthy family norms.

Varieties of Abuse

Abuses that characterize dysfunctional families can include physical abuse, emotional abuse, sexual injury or neglect. Abuse may be blatant, such as one family member striking or screaming at another. Or it can be subtle, as when one person ignores another. Abuse can also be vicarious, such as the inner pain the individual suffers when observing the abuse experienced by his mother, brother or sister.

One form of abuse that is often overlooked because it leaves no visible scars is emotional mistreatment. Here are some examples:

- Giving a child choices that are only negative. Example: "Eat every bite of your dinner or get a spanking."
- Constantly projecting blame onto a child.
- Distorting a child's sense of reality. Example: "Your father

doesn't have a drinking problem. He just works too hard and he's tired."
- Overprotecting a child.
- Blaming others for the child's problem.
- Communicating double messages to the child. Saying, "Yes, I love you," while glaring hatefully at the child only confuses her. (The child will believe the nonverbal message.)

This is not a happy home.

- *Did any of this occur in your home? What about your partner's? If so, how does this affect your relationship?*

Perfectionism

Perfectionism is rarely considered an unhealthy symptom, but it is a common source of many family problems, especially in

≈ Christians are called to live a life of excellence.
Excellence is attainable, perfection is not. ≈

Christian homes. After all, isn't the challenge of the Christian life to be perfect as God is perfect? That word "perfect" in Matthew 5:48 is actually a call to *love* perfectly—as God loves—not a call to an impossible state of perfection. Christians are called to live a life of excellence. Excellence is attainable, perfection is not. Expecting perfect behavior from spouse or children, even in a Christian family, is living in a world of unreality.

A perfectionistic parent conveys his or her standards and expectations through verbal rebukes and corrections, frowns, penetrating glances, smirks and so on, which continually imply, "It's not good enough." Such a parent lives and leads by *oughts, shoulds* and *musts*. These are "torture words" that elevate guilt and lower self-esteem. (More will be said about this in a later chapter.)

- *If perfectionism was a part of your family life, how will it affect your relationships? Have you seen any signs of this in your partner's family or in your partner? Have you discussed this yet?*

Rigidity

Dysfunctional families are characterized by unbending rules and strict lifestyles and belief systems. Life for them is full of compulsions, routines, controlled situations, controlled relationships and unrealistic and unchallenged beliefs. Joy? There is none. Surprises? There are none. Spontaneity? There will be none—unless it is planned! I'm not talking about a personality trait or tendency here, but a way of living that seeks to control life and others.

- *If rigidity was a part of your family life, how will it affect your relationships? What about your partner's family background?*

Silence

Dysfunctional families operate by a gag rule: No talking outside these walls. Don't share family secrets with anyone. Don't ask anyone else for help if you're having a problem. Keep it in the family.

A person who grew up in a home where the gag rule was enforced probably feels he has to handle all of his problems by himself. It's difficult for him to ask for assistance or advice. Openness in the relationship with his partner may be lacking, or there could be a low level of trust. His motto is, "Tough it out by yourself!"

- *If a gag rule was enforced in your family, how will this affect your relationships? Any signs of this in your partner's background? Does your partner ever withdraw or use silence? Do you?*

Repression

A man or woman may have grown up in a family where emotions were controlled and repressed instead of identified and expressed. Emotional repression has been called the "death sentence of a marriage." Anger, sadness, joy and pain, emotions that should be expressed among family members, are buried. The object of the game is to express the feelings that are "appropriate" instead of what you really feel. *Deny reality* and *Disguise your true identity by wearing a mask* are the lessons learned.

Emotions are a very important part of life. Like a pressure valve, they help us interpret and respond to the joys and sorrows of life. Clogging the valve by repressing or denying our feelings leads to physical problems such as ulcers, depression, high blood pressure, headaches and susceptibility to a host of physical ailments. Repressing feelings can trigger overeating, anorexia and bulimia, substance abuse and compulsions of all types. And in a relationship, it's like a slow-growing, terminal cancer.

- *Was repression a part of your family life as a child? What emotions are you comfortable sharing? What emotions or feelings do you wish you could talk about? What about your partner? Is there too much of any emotion coming out at this time in the relationship?*

Triangulation

Have you ever heard of triangulation? No, I'm not talking about the "Bermuda Triangle," that place off the Florida coast where boats and ships seem to disappear. Triangulation refers to a three-way, dysfunctional communication process in the family.

In triangulation, one family member uses another family member as a go-between. Father tells his daughter, Jean, "Go see if your mother is still angry at me. Tell her I love her."

Jean complies with his request, but Mother replies, "Tell your father to get lost!"

How does Jean feel about getting caught in the middle? Perhaps she feels like a failure. She let her father down. Perhaps she fears that her mother is angry at her.

When triangulation is a regular pattern in a family, a child feels used. She becomes involved in problems of which she should have no part. She becomes a guilt collector, experiencing feelings she doesn't need and simply cannot handle. Throughout her life she tries to be a "fixer" or a "rescuer" and can easily carry this tendency into her marriage.

You know, in a sense this *is* like the Bermuda Triangle. Something does disappear—healthy communication!

 • *If this was a part of your history, how do you see it impacting your relationships? Is triangulation a part of your partner's history? Some people think this is normal. It's not!*

Double Messages

A wife asks her husband if he loves her. "Sure, of course I do," he says as he gulps his food while reading the newspaper. Then he spends four hours in front of the TV and goes to bed without saying one more word to her. His words say, "I love you," but his actions say, "I don't care about you at all." It's a double message. The words and actions aren't adding up.

You put your arms around your partner and feel his back stiffen as he subtly tries to pull away. You both say, "I love you," but you also sense the body language saying, "I don't like being close to you." It's a double message.

Remember this: In any face-to-face communication the message has three parts—content, tone of voice and nonverbals or body language. The actual content or words make up only 7 percent of the message. The tone of voice makes up 38 percent, and the nonverbal carries 55 percent of the message. When these three elements of communication don't add up, confusion is the result. Listen to the nonverbals. They say a lot.

Common double messages include: "I love you"/"Don't bother me now." "I love you"/"Get lost." "I need you"/"You're in my way." "Yes, I accept you"/"Why can't you be more like Susan?" Such subtle and conflicting messages are confusing, especially when you hear them as a child. Even as an adult it's painful.

- *If double messages were a regular part of your family life, how will this affect your relationship? Do you see any indication of this occurring now with your partner, either on your part or theirs? If so, now is the time to confront it.*

Lack of Fun

Dysfunctional families are typically unable to loosen up, play and have fun. They're overbalanced on the serious side of life. Their mottos are: "Be Serious." "Work Hard." "You Are What You Do."

When members of this kind of family do engage in play, it usually ends up with someone getting hurt. They don't know when to stop. They've never learned the skills. And humor is used as much to hurt as to have fun. There can be a major conflict in a relationship if one person comes from this background. One partner knows how to have fun, but the other does not.

- *Did you hear any of these messages when you were growing up? Do you know how to play? Does your partner?*

Martyrdom

Some families have a high tolerance for personal abuse and pain. Children hear their parents preaching that others come first, no matter what the personal cost. (There's usually a "poor me" tone to their voice as well.) Children see their parents punish themselves through excessive behaviors such as drinking too much, overworking, overeating or exercising too hard.

Children in a martyrdom family are often challenged by their parents. "Tough it out, son. Big boys don't cry." "You aren't hurt, Jane, so quit that whimpering—or else!" They see themselves as victims, pleasers or martyrs.

If you learned to be a martyr as a child, as an adult you may try to handle weakness by denying yourself pleasure or advantage, or by suppressing your true feelings. Some martyrs actually pride themselves on how much they can bear before the pain becomes intolerable. This is not a spiritual calling! Often such people are eager for you to know what martyrs they are. They know how to push the guilt button.

- *If martyrdom was a part of your upbringing, how will it contribute to your relationship? Will it help or hinder? Will it draw your partner closer or push him or her away? It's something to consider.*

Entanglement

Years ago I was walking on a small island in the middle of a stream in the Grand Teton National Park. As I pushed my way through the undergrowth my foot struck a log and it fell in two. It had rotted out, and inside were hundreds of worms known as night crawlers. They were wiggling and trying to get out of the light.

Ever alert for good fish bait, I plunged my hand into the mass of worms and pulled up a gigantic ball of these squirming critters. As I looked closer, I could see that many were intertwined and wrapped around one another. It was hard to find where one began and the other left off.

That tangled mass reminded me of some families I've seen. Only they're tangled up in other ways. They're emotionally and relationally entangled in each other's lives. Individual identities are enmeshed. There are no clear-cut boundaries between each member. Everybody pokes his nose into everybody else's business. Mom makes Dad's problems her problems, Dad makes the kids' problems his problems, and so on. Everyone shares everyone else's problems.

In enmeshed families, if one family member is unhappy, the whole family is blue, and everybody blames everybody else for the state they're in. It's as though the whole family is sitting together on a giant swing. When one goes up, the others go up. When one goes down, the others go down. Nobody thinks or feels for himself.

The lack of proper boundaries can be very destructive in a new marriage. What do you think will happen when you marry?

Will entangled members of your family of origin back off? Probably not. They'll just reach out with their tentacles like a giant squid and try to engulf your partner as well as the relationship. It's not a pretty sight.

Roles Within a Dysfunctional Family

People who come from dysfunctional families often develop specific roles. As a child in this kind of family grows up he probably "plays" a role or combination of roles in his interaction with

≈ A role is a mask, a child's way of coping with the pain of not having his needs met by his family. Are you or your partner still playing roles in your relationship? ≈

other family members. The role is not his true self, but an identity he takes on or is forced to play in order to get along. It's called "survival time." Unfortunately such people usually continue to play roles as they move through adulthood.

What does a role accomplish? Often it's a mask, a way of coping with the pain of not having needs met by other family members. If a person didn't receive recognition or affirmation for who he was, then he probably took on a role to get the attention he needed.

In the following discussion of roles commonly assumed in many families, think about any you may have played. Who else in your family played roles? Look at your partner as well. Is role-playing continuing in your current relationship?

The Doer

A doer plays the role of a very busy person who provides most of the maintenance functions in the family. Known as supremely responsible, she makes sure that bills are paid and people are fed, clothed and chauffeured. Of course these tasks need to be completed even in a functional home, but the doer spends almost all her time and energy doing them.

In "doer" families, the motto is, "Give it to her and it will get done." If you try to do it, she acts like an overprotective nation trying to repel an invader from her borders! She will find ways to get that responsibility away from you. Was there such a doer in your family?

Doers have an overdeveloped sense of responsibility. It drives them. They get satisfaction from accomplishments. Why? Because other family members like what the doers do, and in one way or another encourage them to "keep it up." Doers are applauded—and why not? It lets the other family members off the hook.

Doers often feel tired, isolated, ignored and used. But the recognition received for what they do keeps them going.

Sometimes the doer is also the enabler in the family. In most families the doer is one of the parents, often the mother.

Do you choose doers for close relationships? Do you tend to be a doer yourself? What about your partner? On the "Doer Meter" below, indicate where you see both yourself and your partner, and discuss it together.

0..5..10
Doer? What's That?   Partial Doer   Full-Blown Doer

The Enabler

Enablers are providers. They nurture the family emotionally and relationally and provide the family with a sense of belonging. They're the peacemakers who preserve family unity at all costs. Their goal is to avoid conflicts and help everyone get along.

As noble as such goals may be, enablers have an ulterior motive. What they do is driven by their fears: the fear that family members cannot survive without each other, and their own fear of being abandoned.

Enabling behavior usually happens so gradually that the person who plays this role is often unaware of it. He is constrained to do whatever is necessary to keep the family on an even keel.

Unfortunately, the enabler will even excuse or defend a family member's dysfunctional behavior in order to keep the peace. She sells out for peace. For example, the wife of an alcoholic may cover for him and deny that he has a problem in an attempt to hold the family together. But, sadly, enabling behavior also allows the enabled family member to continue his destructive behavior.

Do you see any signs or hints of this in your current relationship?

Sometimes enablers can be unpleasant. They may resort to anger, nagging or sarcasm to manipulate family members to do what they want.

Some Christian enablers even misuse their faith in family crises. Instead of doing something constructive about a problem, they sit around waiting for God to intervene with a miracle.

- *Who are the enablers you know? Can you think of a situation or pattern when you played the role of enabler for your partner? Does your partner play this role? Can you think of a healthier way of responding rather than enabling?*

The Loner

Loners cope with family pressures by physically or emotionally withdrawing. They avoid intimate contact with family members, preferring to stay out of sight, either in their room or away from the home. When they're with others they don't participate much.

Obviously loners are meeting some needs of their own. But they may also meet the need other family members may have for autonomy and separateness. They may even reinforce this tendency. But the way it's done is unhealthy for everyone.

A loner may not be close to either parent. Usually he is quite passive and shows little anger. The loner rarely distinguishes himself in any way and often goes unnoticed. It's almost as though he is "out of sight and out of mind." Even his moments of accomplishment are often overshadowed by others who attract the limelight.

This is the lost child, the forgotten one in the family. Many lost children grow up to be lost adults. Sadly, they never find their place in life, living entirely in denial. You can imagine what happens when they marry. Perhaps they marry because they allowed a rescuer to rescue them. Perhaps they portrayed another image of who they were to attract someone. I've seen a few of these in my counseling office over the years. They reminded me of hermits, yet they were married. They contributed very little relationally, and their spouses were totally frustrated.

- *Does anyone you know come to mind when you think of a loner?*

The Hero
Everyone seems to like having a hero around—someone whose success and achievement brings recognition and prestige to the family. Heroes get most of the attention in a family, and they usually love it! They're addicted to pleasing others: parents, teachers, employers, God. When the family star successfully fulfills his parents' dreams, he often accepts their dreams as his own.

I've seen pastors and doctors who chose their careers not because it was their calling, but because their parents wanted them to. And the acknowledgement received for their deeds builds up the self-esteem of their family members. ("That's my *son*, the doctor!")

There is a personal cost for playing this role, and it's astronomical. Heroes strive for achievement at the cost of sacrificing their own well-being. They fail to develop a well-integrated personal value system because their focus is always on pleasing others. When their values are attacked they may fold under the pressure.

Heroes tend to be very critical, so friendships are difficult to come by. They may even be very popular, but still feel alone. Feelings are guarded closely. They live with the fear that if honest feelings are revealed their weakness will be obvious.

Heroes are often the oldest children in families. As such, they often become enablers by denying themselves in order to care for younger siblings. This pleases their parents. But the results later in adulthood can be painful. (By the way, what's your position in the birth order of your family?)

Heroes eventually burn out because of their strenuous efforts to be good through overachieving. As the hero's halo gradually disintegrates, he begins to behave in ways that are totally foreign to him. A hero often turns out to be the complete opposite of his assumed role, trading his "Superman" cloak for a demon's cape.

- *Do you or your partner tend to play the role of hero? What type of future spouse might heroes tend to choose? To attract?*

The Mascot

Mascots are the family clowns. They bring humor into the family through play, fun, even silliness. Clowns are always joking and cutting up, especially when confronted by difficult situations. And some of their antics come at inappropriate times. A fun-loving nature is a great cover for feelings of pain and isolation.

The mascot's humor brings the attention he is unable to get in other ways. If you're involved with a mascot, it's easy to be so entertained by him that you miss the pain he carries, as well as the potential problems a clown can bring to a relationship. You'll find times when you want him to "get serious," but to no avail.

- *Do you or your partner tend to hide behind a clown's humor?*

The Manipulator

Manipulators are the controllers in families. They can be extremely clever. They learn early how to get others to do what they want them to do. They use seduction, charm, false illness, the appearance of weakness—every trick in the book—to get their way.

Sometimes it's difficult to identify a manipulator unless you get to know them very well and observe them with their family or at work. They've done this so long they've refined their methods.

- *Any signs that you or your partner try to manipulate each other?*

The Critic

The critic is the family faultfinder. Just what every family needs. She sees the water glass as half-empty instead of half-full.

Critics are characterized by complaining, sarcasm and teasing that inflicts pain. They'd rather use their energy tearing others down than building them up. Critics aren't very pleasant to be around, but some families have to endure them.

- *How does constant criticism affect a relationship? Do you or your partner need to be less critical?*

The Scapegoat

The scapegoat is the family victim—the blame collector. Everyone else in the family looks at the scapegoat and says, "If it weren't for him, our family would be all right." If the scapegoat tries to change his role, other family members won't let him off the hook. As long as he's around, they have someone to blame for their own irresponsibility.

Even though a scapegoat doesn't seem to care what is going on, he's usually the most sensitive person in the family. He's especially sensitive to the pain he sees in the family, so the stress he feels through what they do is often acted out. His actions may be a cry to the rest of the family to do something about the pain that's happening in the home.

When the scapegoat is a child, he feels responsible for keeping his parents' marriage together. If he senses problems between them, he may misbehave to unify them in attacking him.

A scapegoat may be sought as a spouse by a victim who is seeking someone to help her continue her own role because she is so accustomed to it. Victims often look to scapegoats to rescue them from their own sense of guilt.

- *Do you know any scapegoats? How would they respond in a marriage?*

Daddy's Little Princess/Mommy's Little Man

Some parents refer to their children using these terms. Often they do so in fun. But with some families these terms are not harmless nicknames. They're subtle and intense forms of emotional abuse.

A father may thrust his daughter into the role of little princess as a substitute for his wife in some ways. This dad is afraid of getting his emotional needs met by his wife, so he elevates his daughter to princess status and uses her to gain emotional fulfillment.[2] A mother may do the same with her son.

Being a parent's little princess or prince may make the child feel special. Unfortunately, however, the youngster is denied his childhood because the parent demands adult responses from him. The boundaries of the child are not respected; they're violated. When the child grows up, in many cases he becomes the victim of physical or emotional abuse by other adults. It's a potentially dangerous situation.

Not many people would want to be married to a prince or princess. You might be treated like a servant.

- *What would it be like to be married to a prince or princess?*

The Saint

A child playing the role of saint is expected to express the family's spirituality. It may not be directly stated, but is certainly implied. For example, parents may expect their daughter to go

into full-time Christian work. But under the pressure of con-
forming to this role, she may end up denying her sexuality. These
normal desires seem so unspiritual. Her worth as a person
becomes dependent upon following the course of action laid out
by her parents. The church and others may reinforce the parents'
message.

A young man may learn to give the outward appearance of
being spiritual, but it could be just a cover-up. He may actually
be repressing anger, and he may be hesitant to be totally honest
with his partner for fear of tainting his image. In marriage all
these cover-ups are unwrapped.

- *Do you or your partner tend to cover up your faults?*
  What are the dangers of "sainthood" in a relationship?

Why Play a Role?

It's important to remember that the reason these roles are
unhealthy is because that's all they are—*roles*. In a healthy family, no one is pigeonholed into one slot and expected to remain
there the rest of his or her life. In a healthy family you're allowed
to be you. Your own personality is allowed and encouraged to
come to the forefront. Other family members encourage you to
develop and express your individuality. Mother and father are
united in their beliefs and values. One parent does not secretly pit
children against the other parent by asking them to play a role.

You may be wondering, "Why would anyone want to continue playing a role, especially those that are so unhealthy for the
individual or the family?"

It's not usually a matter of choice. People adopt a role as a
means of defense, a way to deal with family difficulties and pressures. That role becomes part of their personality. As they grow
into adulthood, they continue to utilize that role to deal with
problems in the world outside the family.

It's true that they may realize to some extent the pain of the
role, but it's usually easier to accept that pain than to face the

world without the defensive armor of the role.[3]

Where do you go from here, especially if you've discovered that this chapter has spoken to you about your own life or the life of your partner? Some readers may find help through counseling, whereas others could benefit from further reading.[4]

When you marry, you want a healthy relationship—with a real person. It takes time and a thorough knowledge of yourself and the other person to discern whether he or she is playing a role.

Notes

1. Sara Hines Martin, *Healing for Adult Children of Alcoholics* (Nashville: Broadman & Holman Publishers, 1988), p. 34.
2. H. Norman Wright, *Always Daddy's Girl* (Ventura, Calif.: Regal Books, 1989), pp. 141-82. Adapted.
3. Hines Martin, op. cit.
4. See especially *Family Cycles* by Dr. Wm. Lee Carter; *Love Is a Choice* by Dr. Robert Hemfelt, Dr. Frank Minirth and Dr. Paul Meier, especially Part 5, "The Ten Stages of Recovery"; *Your Family Voyage* by Roger Hillerstrom; and *Making Peace with Your Past* by H. Norman Wright.

The Chemistry of Attraction —or Is It Sex?

≈

*Why do people often get involved sexually
before marriage? And why does it so often
damage the relationship?*

Why are you attracted to another person? "We knew we were right for one another," couples say. "There's this chemistry between us." And that's probably true. The problem is that there are different kinds of chemistry, or different elements. If two of the elements are there but five are missing, you end up with an incomplete bond.

Actually I prefer the word "connection" over chemistry. Physical chemistry is all right. It's good. And it needs to be there because it generates desire. But by itself it tends to be a transient resident.

Male-Female Differences

It's easy for a man to be turned on physically whether he plans to be or not. It just happens. Men tend to see sex everywhere and in everything. Sexual thoughts flow in and out of men's minds all day long. According to one report on male sexuality, 16 percent of conservative Christian men surveyed said they thought about it hourly. Although men slow down their sexual thinking during their 40s and 50s, they still think about it several times a day.

Men also tend to dream about sex three times as often as women, and their dreams rarely involve their own wives. Women object to the notion that the majority of men admit to fantasizing about other women for sexual stimulation. Fantasizing seems to be intriguing, and many men need some kind of fantasy (whether a real person or not) to become sexually aroused.

Men think about sex more often than they like to admit. They think about it during the day, when they go to bed and when they wake up. Archibald Hart describes it well:

> Sure, the average man thinks of other things, like football and politics, but eventually all mental roads lead back to this one central fixation: sex. There are times when the obsession fades and even vanishes. Give him a golf bag or a fishing trip. He'll forget about sex for a while. But sooner or later, like a smoldering fire, it will flare up again. Strong, urgent, forceful and impatient, the sex drive dominates the mind and body of every healthy male. Like it or not, that's the way it is.[1]

Another problem contributing to men's sexual struggles is the lack of understanding many women show concerning the male sex drive. I do not mean to be diverting the blame or responsibility, but many women just don't understand this basic masculine need. Women are not as interested, obsessed or compulsive about it.

Some women are either vain about their looks or they simply enjoy tantalizing men. When they dress provocatively to attract one man, all men notice. Men are aroused by proximity, perfume and revealing clothing.

Sex has a different meaning for men than for women in love

relationships. Most women give sex to achieve emotional closeness, while too many men view sex as the only way to be close.

Tenderness, touching, talking and sex go hand-in-hand for a woman. Many men think sex is sufficient, especially if they do not know how to achieve intimacy in other ways. It is easy for men to substitute sex for sharing. Sex is an expression of emotion; however, for many men it often serves as a substitute for emotion. And there are differences in lustful thoughts as well. Consider what one author has said.

> Often men and women experience different kinds of lust. Most men battle with impulsive lust based on physical attractiveness. Most women battle selective lust, desiring men whom they consider special. Men are led into sexual sin by lusting after women's bodies, most often beginning with the eye gates. Women are led into sexual sin by lusting after men's attentiveness, most often beginning with the ear gates.
>
> Men fall into lust because of the enticement of physical pleasure. Lustful male fantasies prompt a physical stimulation that raises his voltage. Women fall into lust because of the enticement of emotional pleasure. Female lust most often takes the form of mental fantasy about romance with drama, a love affair with excitement or a triangle with intrigue. Lustful female fantasies cause emotional stimulation that likewise raises her voltage. Most men are first tempted by physical attraction while most women seem more vulnerable to emotional appeal. However, it is also true that some men find emotional attraction a powerful pull upon them and some women feel strong sexual urges from the visual sight of a well-built male. The Christian who finds both kinds of urges, physical and emotional, stimulated by the opposite sex must be doubly careful. When channeled in the right direction, this man or woman is often warm, attractive and caring—wonderful qualities in a Christian. Outside of

Christ's control, however, this same person can fall easily
into sexual immorality.[2]

Premature Physical Involvement

So we all know that men are very interested in sex. Many times
a woman does not want to get that involved physically, but ends
up doing so. Many want to wait for marriage because of their
faith or their value system or for other personal reasons.
Unfortunately, many of them don't wait.

Why? What are some of the reasons? Laurie Langford dis-
cusses this in her book, *If It's Love You Want, Why Settle for
Just Sex?*[3] Langford suggests that a woman may go out with a man
who basically isn't right for her because of timing, loneliness or
lust. Often the red flags are obvious but ignored. The potential for
a deep connection just isn't there. She may be aware of this ini-
tially but hopes a quality relationship will develop. Rarely does
that happen.

Not Sticking to Standards

A woman may not be aware of what her standards are. I grew up
in a landlord situation. My parents owned four houses. But
before a person or family was accepted as a renter, they had to
provide references, put up a security deposit, and submit to a
credit check. Then they had to agree to follow some rules in
order to stay, such as no smoking inside, no pets and no wild
drunken parties.

When couples care for each other they usually express their
feelings of caring through some kind of physical contact. But just
how far should you go in expressing your care and love? What is
right and what is wrong? What is proper and what isn't? Are there
any standards or guidelines?

It's amazing that some people who would follow rules for
renting accommodations don't stick to them when it comes to
sexuality. The chart below depicts various types of sexual expression and the standards of four different couples. It indicates the

different ways people express their affection to each other.

Look at the abbreviations and their meanings. The first couple engages in all of the various sexual activities very rapidly. The second couple leaves only sexual intercourse for marriage. Such

≈ Too many women become sexually involved with a man without knowing his values, intentions or even whether he is marriage material. ≈

people are sometimes referred to as "technical virgins." The third couple has gone as far as French kissing prior to marriage, and the last couple has engaged in kissing but left everything else for marriage.

Sexual Behavior

Key:

L = Look	K = Strong kiss
T = Touch	FrK = French kiss
h = Holding hands lightly	B = Fondling of the breasts
H = Constantly holding hands	SO = Fondling of sexual organs
k = light kiss	SI = Sexual intercourse

	Friendship	Dating	Exclusive Dating	Engagement	Marriage
Couple 1	L, T	h, H, k, K, FrK, B	SO, SI		
Couple 2	L, T	h, H	k, K	FrK, B, SO	SI
Couple 3	L, T	h, H, k	K	FrK	B, SO, SI
Couple 4	L, T	h, H	k, K	K	FrK, B, SO, S
You					

Where are you on this chart? Take some time and fill in the chart for yourself on another piece of paper. If you are currently in a relationship, ask your partner to read this and make his or her own decisions as well. How will you maintain your standards? How will you explain it to the other person in a non-apologetic and non-defensive manner?

Too many women become sexually involved with a man without knowing his values, intentions or, very bluntly, whether he is marriage material. Too many women give too freely, which kills the love potential with a man. When I was in the Air National Guard Reserves, I ran into man after man who slept with women as soon as they could, but when they talked about getting married some day, they all said they wanted to marry a virgin! Interesting.

Don't wait until you get in a relationship to determine your standards. Emotions and physical desire can be confusing.

Defining Mr. or Mrs. Right

Another reason for premature sexual involvement is not really knowing what you want for a spouse. Without a goal in mind you can end up drifting or taking potluck. What do you want in a relationship? What's your definition of a good spouse?

I've encouraged men and women to write out a description of the characteristics or qualities of the kind of person they would want to spend the rest of their lives with. Put them in a list form. Call the first list "Must Haves." These are the essentials, about which there can be no negotiation. Call a second list, "Would Like to Have but Can Live Without Them." And you may want to make one last list labeled "Never," for those characteristics that would prevent you from allowing a person to get one foot in the door.

What you come up with reflects your values and your dreams. Many have something like this in mind, but seeing it in black and white puts it into a different dimension altogether.

As you look at your list, ask yourself: Does anyone like this exist? You'll need to be flexible and adjust as you go on your search. For additional assistance in this project, see the book *Finding Your Perfect Mate* (Harvest House).

Walk, Talk and Dress for the Part!

Another reason for early physical involvement is the message that a woman sends out via what she says, how she dresses and how she behaves. (Remember, I'm drawing on a woman author for some of these suggestions.) Women do like to dress well, and they enjoy attention from men. But men can misinterpret your message. Consider the presentation you make. To maintain your standards and your Christian testimony, evaluate how you dress, act and talk in light of the passage, "Do not be conformed to this world" (Rom. 12:2, *NASB*).

Consider the Consequences

Not thinking about the consequences of sex is another reason for early physical involvement. Some people tend to live for the moment. The fulfillment of a need, especially if we're starving, tends to short-circuit reason.

Raging hormones often accompany a high need for attention, security, closeness and affection. An unplanned step into a sexual relationship is quite easy under these conditions. Sex is used to not only fulfill these needs but to connect after a disagreement. And sometimes the physical response is a reflection of an addictive personality.

Some use a sexual relationship to accelerate the growth of love. Those who have low impulse control or want immediate results will bypass the time and effort it takes for a true love relationship to really develop.

Many women struggle with the fear of losing the man, especially if dating relationships are infrequent as you grow older. It's impossible to have a healthy relationship of any kind based on fear. Trying to keep a man with sex won't work. If this seems to be the only course open to you, you need to hear a blunt message: This isn't the right man for you. And who is to say that having sex will keep a man? Just because a man is aggressive in pursuing a woman sexually doesn't mean she's all that important to him! Many women are left wondering after a sexual relationship why the man doesn't call.

Failing to consider consequences is especially dangerous in these times when the risk of sexually transmitted diseases is higher than it has ever been. More of these disease can be fatal than ever before.

Mistaken Perceptions

Some sexual involvement results from a woman's having too low a perception of herself, or too high a perception of the relationship.

Lack of self-confidence and low self-esteem are common reasons for sexual involvement. Some don't feel worthy of being pure sexually. They feel that all they have to offer is the physical.

The fact is that having a man in your life won't solve the problem of a low self-image. If anything, sexual involvement will compound the problem, especially if you base your feelings about yourself on how the man responds.

A final reason the physical relationship can get out of hand is believing you have more of a relationship than you really do. Sometimes a relationship is in the heart and mind of one person and not the other. It's also easy to misread and misinterpret actions and comments. You need to look at what the other person does and says as an outside objective observer.

There are other reasons for a woman becoming involved sexually, but perhaps these can help you evaluate your responses, and also serve as a warning for future involvement. To summarize, the best way to maintain a pure relationship is to:

1. Identify your values in advance.
2. List all the negative results of premarital sexual involvement. If you need help in this area, see the book *Why Wait* by Josh McDowell and Dick Day for a listing of 26 reasons to wait.
3. Write out your definition of the kind of spouse you want.
4. Dress appropriately in light of these standards, consider the consequences of not following them, and check

your perceptions of yourself and of each other's signals.

5. Be open about your standards, and if your relationship is developing, establish a covenant of sexual conduct together. Commit it to the Lord through prayer, sign it, and become accountable together to two other couples.

Sharing Your Commitment

Some couples find it helpful to discuss the ground rules of their relationship with a mature friend or mentor, and with their significant other as well. The following statement is a covenant one man made with his fiancée.

I vow to you to treat you as my friend in the Lord. Because I know you desire that my affections for you be channeled toward your personality, I will put all conscious effort into assuring that my affections for you are directed toward you as a person, not simply toward your body.

What I have written down here is an outline of definite actions to be taken, and definite situations for us to avoid in order to honor this vow.

1. Pray concerning this one specific area for 5 to 10 minutes a day during our prayer times.
2. Spend 15 minutes a day when we are together sharing with each other what the best part of our day was.
3. The next time we are together, we will both bow before the Lord and spread out this petition before Him.
4. Judging from the past, what we shall not do is to find ourselves in any room with the doors closed, especially after your parents have gone to bed.
5. In those times when we will hug and kiss, then I will take the responsibility to notice when we need to separate ourselves, probably spatially. This will be interpreted not as rejection, but as necessity for the growth of the relationship.

6. You can anticipate that I will channel some of my strong urges into writing, because I know you like this.
7. While on extended drives there will be no touching above the knees, nor below the shoulders.

Perhaps this can serve as a sample in case you decide to create your own statement of commitment and intent.

≈ Sex in a single relationship is a roadblock, or barrier, to genuine intimacy. ≈

How Singles Sex Inhibits Intimacy

Sex in a single relationship is a roadblock, or barrier, to genuine intimacy. When sex is involved before a foundation of love has been built, more likely than not it limits the chances of building the type of love and relationship that a couple is looking for.

"Sex out of synch" can cause a woman, especially, to lose her balance, feel insecure, lose control of her emotions and alter her judgement. It can create confusion and uncertainty as to how both individuals feel, and keep her from digging deep to fully get to know the other person. For some, it lowers their sense of self-esteem and could lead to an addictive relationship. This makes it difficult to gain an accurate reading on yourself, the other person and the relationship.

Physical chemistry needs fuel or a backup system, and that comes from the other elements of a relationship. You can have passion (for a while) without the other elements, but then emptiness will develop. You need the full range of emotional chemistry or connection to create lasting affection. You need a mental connection or chemistry to keep interest and growth alive. Social chemistry generates companionship between a couple. The spiritual connection not only enhances love but infuses the other connective elements.

Think of a relationship as a chemistry lab. You're engaged in an experiment. You don't know whether your experiments will be successful but that's all right. You're there to learn. Sometimes what you create will be a totally new discovery—a real surprise. And on other occasions the results are tossed down the drain.

Perhaps a diagram will help.

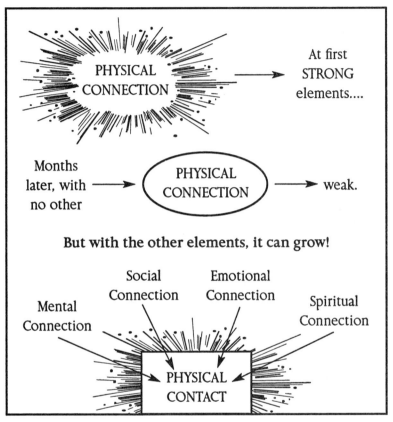

Friends, Lovers...or Both?

You may be asking, "What is a better basis than sex for building a relationship?"

It's simple: *friendship.*

Referring again to the New Testament's language of love, friendship is the important element of *philia,* as distinct from *eros* or attraction, which includes erotic love.

When you fall in love with someone who was first a good friend, you have one of the best bases for a marriage. That's a strong statement! But I believe it's true. The qualities that go into the building of a friendship are the qualities that contribute to a lasting marriage. Ask any dating couple if they are friends and you know what you'll hear: "Of course we are. We're the best of friends!" The reality is that all too few understand the factors that make up a deep, lasting friendship.

Do you know what it means to be a friend? I mean a real friend? Think about this. A friend is...

...more than an acquaintance. Acquaintances are the bit players in the movie of your life; they needn't be cast with care, but they must be noticed and treated with dignity because they are the stars of their own movie.[4]

It's been suggested that while a person makes 500 to 2,500 acquaintances each year, he or she has fewer than seven personal friends. Acquaintances are transient relationships that pass in and out of our lives.

A friend is more than a confederate. Although a confederate is sometimes mistaken for a friend, a confederate is really only an "exchange" friend. Confederates get together because it suits each other's purposes. They're a symbolic pair, united only because they want something from each other.

Friendship is more than being a companion. You can hire a companion. Friendship is like a relationship without self-serving rules.

Walter Winchell said, "A friend is someone who walks in when the rest of the world walks out." They stick with you.

Do these reflections on friendship describe your romantic interest?

The value of a friendship cannot be overestimated. Jesus said:

No longer do I call you slaves, for the slave does not know what his master is doing; but I have called you friends, for all things that I have heard from My Father I have made known to you (John 15:15, *NASB*).

One way to test whether a relationship includes friendship is to take away the romantic connections. What is left? With many couples, not much. Have you thought about the ingredients of a friendship?

C. S. Lewis suggested that we picture lovers face-to-face, but friends side-by-side. Their eyes look ahead. In a friendship, something other than the other person brings them together, such as a common goal or object on which both individuals focus and which both pursue. It could be a hobby, a job, tennis, music, serving on a worship team, etc. But it's outside of themselves. It's this common interest they focus on rather than the relationship.[5]

A friend is someone who knows you thoroughly and still likes you. He or she knows your strengths and weaknesses. A friend is a person who stands by you. He is on your side of the struggle.

Proverbs 17:17, *NASB*, says, "A friend loves at all times, and a brother is born for adversity." Loving at all times—that's hard. It's

≈ The difference between passionate love and friendship is that passionate love thrives on deprivation, frustration and a high arousal level. That sounds more negative than positive! ≈

easier to do it frequently, but at "all times"? Durability is a characteristic of a true friendship.

Proverbs 18:24 says, "A man of many friends comes to ruin, but there is a friend who sticks closer than a brother." Not only durability but adhesion is a quality of friendship.

Friendship love has been described as "companionate love." This may be defined as a strong bond, including a tender attachment and enjoyment of the other's company. It is *not* characterized by wild passion and constant excitement, although these feelings may be experienced from time to time.

Did you get that? Some people have to have those wild feelings or it's not a relationship. The main difference between passionate and companionate love is that the former thrives on deprivation, frustration, a high arousal level and abstinence. All that sounds more negative than positive! Companionate love, on the other hand, thrives on contact and requires time to develop and mature.[6]

Further to Being a Friend

Since friendship is so important, let's explore it further. Lou and Colleen Evans describe the quality of friendship needed in a marriage:

> A friend is someone with whom I can share my ideas and philosophies, someone with whom I can grow intellectually.
> My friend is one who hears my cry of pain, who senses my struggle, who shares any lows as well as my highs.
> When I am troubled, my friend stands not only by my side, but also stands apart, looking at me with some objectivity. My friend does not always say I am right, because sometimes I am not.[7]

If you were to ask others what a close friend is like, you would likely hear some of the following responses:

A friend knows you inside and out and still likes you.

A friend understands you and appreciates you even though he has different views.

A friend is faithful and loyal, and you can trust her explicitly.

With a friend what you share is deep, not just opinions or observations.

In friendship, you risk being hurt because you make yourself vulnerable.

It is difficult to imagine a lifelong marriage in which these ingredients are lacking. Unfortunately, they exist in some marriages for a brief time but in others not at all.

Friendship as Loyalty

An in-depth friendship reflects loyalty. Loyalty means the person sticks with you—regardless! "A friend loves at all times, and a brother is born for adversity" (Prov. 17:17). The book of Proverbs, with its practical principles for everyday living, speaks about the fleeting nature of a friendship built on the external qualities that many are pursuing today: wealth, position or power.

> Wealth brings many friends, but a poor man's friend deserts him. A false witness will not go unpunished, and he who pours out lies will not go free. Many curry favor with a ruler, and everyone is the friend of a man who gives gifts. A poor man is shunned by all his relatives—how much more do his friends avoid him! (Prov. 19:4-7).

When you are loyal you can be trusted with information that is sensitive. Your friend knows it will be kept as a sacred trust. When a confidence is violated, it's a deathblow to a relationship.

Proverbs states, "A brother offended is harder to be won than a strong city" (18:19, NASB). Also, "Many a man proclaims his own loyalty, but who can find a trustworthy man?" (20:6, NASB).

In what way is loyalty demonstrated in your relationship? In what ways could it be improved?

In-Depth Sharing

A second quality of real friendship is in-depth sharing. This does not develop overnight. Deep sharing means an eagerness to listen as well as to talk, accepting rather than being a judge. The listening required in this kind of friendship is the kind that prevents your thinking about what you're going to say when the other person quits talking!

No one has described this depth of sharing as well as John

Powell in an older book, *Why Am I Afraid to Tell You Who I Am?* He writes about the five levels of conversation.

> The lowest level of conversation, the weakest response is the cliché level. This is the level of no real sharing. The polite responses which take no thought nor contain any substance do not connect one person to another.
>
> The next level is reporting the facts and information about others. You still don't expose much of yourself. You give nothing of yourself, and that's what you invite from others...nothing.
>
> The third level is sharing your ideas and judgements. You still censor what you say since you want to be accepted, but you're willing to reveal some of your ideas, judgments and decisions.
>
> The fourth level is sharing your feelings. It's the feelings underlying what you believe that are important. For two people to know who one another really is, this level must occur.
>
> The ultimate level of conversation is peak communication. From time to time, two individuals will achieve this level of total openness, vulnerability and honesty. Difficult? Yes. Risky? Yes. Rewarding? Yes![8]

What topics can you share deeply with your partner? What would you like to share, but find difficult to do so?

The Fun of Friendship

A friend is someone who is fun to be with. Friends enjoy each other. They laugh, joke, kid around and have common interests.

Friends can be spontaneous. They're willing to try what the other enjoys, but allow each other to say, after trying it, that it's not for them. They enjoy searching until they find something in common.

A friendship is stimulating—you cause one another to grow emotionally, mentally and spiritually. You're challenged to new ways of thinking and growth. "As iron sharpens irons, so one man sharpens another" (Prov. 27:17). You stimulate each other to do the best you can.

How do you and your partner have fun together? In what way has your partner caused you to grow? In what way have you caused your partner to grow?

Friendship and Accountability
A friend holds us accountable. If a friendship is real, the other person can help point out areas in our life where growth or change is needed. We may not like what we hear, often because it may be true; but true friends are able to give and receive correction. "Faithful are the wounds of a friend, but the kisses of an enemy are deceitful" (Prov. 27:6, NKJV).

Obviously caution and sensitivity are needed in this regard:

Friendship is not a hunting license for special weakness. When correction occurs, however, this exchange between close friends will strengthen, rather than threaten, an already strong friendship. There is assurance in knowing that a friend will help us grow and develop. The Holy Spirit corrects us daily, but we may not be sensitive to that correction. So the Spirit may choose to use a friend to point out the error.[9]

Friendship is also made up of self-sacrifice. It costs you to go out of your way to help your friend without resentment. You may be "put out" doing something for them but you don't *feel* put out. Although friendship is *philia* love, the kind of love that undergirds *philia* is *agape*, which is a sacrificial love.

This kind of love is expressed in two ways—actions and words. Some people express friendship more easily in actions, others in words. In a friendship you work on your weakest area of expression and run the risk of doing what is most difficult for you to do. Not only does the relationship grow, but so do you.

In what way have you sacrificed for your partner? In what way has he or she sacrificed for you?

Friendship as Encouragement

A friendship is characterized by mutual encouragement. It builds you up rather than tearing you down. When you encourage people you inspire them to continue on a chosen course. You give courage and confidence. Encouragement is accepting others as having worth and dignity. It validates that what they are doing makes sense. It lets them know, "You can count on me." You find something of value to recognize when everyone else has despaired.

As Christians we don't really have a choice as to whether we encourage others or not. It's not our decision to make. Scripture states that others will know that we are Christians by the love we show for one another. And one of the ways we reflect this love is by being an encourager.

In 1 Thessalonians 5:11 Paul wrote, "Therefore encourage one another and build each other up, just as in fact you are doing." "Encourage" here is from the Greek word *parakaleo*, which carries the idea of being "called alongside" another person to help, console, comfort and cheer up. It also means to "stimulate another person to the ordinary duties of life." This process includes elements of understanding, redirecting of thoughts and a general shifting of focus from the negative to the positive.

In verse 14 Paul tells us to encourage the timid—those who are discouraged and ready to give up. It's a matter of lending your faith and hope to the person until their own develops. This can happen frequently in a friendship.

We also see from this verse that encouragement often takes the form of concrete help. This contains the idea of taking interest in, being devoted to, rendering assistance or holding up spiritually and emotionally. In the context of 1 Thessalonians 5:14, it seems to refer to those who are incapable of helping themselves. There are times when all of us hit these valleys. At such times there's nothing like the helping hand of a friend to keep us going. Encouragement serves us like the concrete pilings of a structural support.

In a Christian friendship there is one additional element—

that of being spiritually challenged. You're able to discuss spiritual issues, pray for one another and grow with the help of your partner.

As you consider these elements of friendship, which ones are the strongest in your relationships? Which need to be strengthened?[10]

Notes

1. Archibald Hart, *The Sexual Man* (Dallas, Tex.: Word Publishing, 1994), p. 5.
2. Charles Mylander, *Running the Red Lights* (Ventura, Calif.: Regal Books, 1986), pp. 53,54.
3. Laurie Langford, *If It's Love You Want, Why Settle for Just Sex?* (Rocklin, Calif.: Prima Publishing, 1996), pp. 3, 15. Adapted.
4. Letty Coltin Pogrebin, *Among Friends* (New York: McGraw-Hill Co., 1987), p. 87.
5. Joshua Harris, *I Kissed Dating Goodbye* (Sisters, Oreg.: Multnomah Books, 1997), p. 128. Adapted.
6. Bernard I. Morstein, *Paths to Marriage* (Newbury Park, Calif.: Sage Publications, 1986), p. 110. Adapted.
7. Colleen and Louis Evans, Jr., *My Lover, My Friend* (Grand Rapids: Fleming H. Revell, 1976), pp. 121-123.
8. John Powell, S.J., *Why Am I Afraid to Tell You Who I Am?* (Chicago: Argus Communications, 1969), pp. 54-62. Adapted.
9. Jerry and Mary White, *Friends and Friendship* (Colorado Springs: NavPress, 1982), p. 79.
10. Ibid., pp. 50-95. Adapted.

Twelve Steps to a Lasting Relationship

≈

From the first glance across a crowded room
to intimate contact in a marriage, wise couples
respect the sequence of the stages of a
developing relationship.

Have you ever heard of the "12 Steps of Intimate Behavior"? No, I'm not talking about a 12-step recovery program of some kind. (Although some would say, "Yes, it is—it's recovering from years of being single!")

Years ago Dr. Desmond Morris, in his book *Intimate Behavior,* described the patterns of human intimacy. Think of these as 12 steps progressing up a ladder.

From Eye to Body
Step one is the step from *eye to body.* This is the look or glance that's involved in checking out another person. I've seen it in singles meetings. So have you. In fact, you probably participated. If the eyes of everyone there had laser beams, the room would

be a mass of light beams going every which way as the "checking-out-everyone" looks crisscross the room.

The glance takes in the other person's characteristics such as sex, size, shape, age, coloring, dress style, etc. It's not that you have an objective check list that you're going through one by one (although some personality types may). The looks are more like evaluative glances, as though you had some scanning device that registers "Yes" or "No."

This is a very important step for some people. They won't progress unless their rating scale registers a definite *Yes—Go for it!* Others will think, *OK, we've passed the first step. Perhaps we'll look further.* Often this is just one person noticing the other. It's not necessarily mutual.

This first evaluative look is all some people need. Their response is, *I think I'm in love.* Sometimes it's more like being "in lust," especially if this occurs around the pool or at the beach. Some couples make their decision to get together based solely upon physical attraction (especially younger couples). And since their basis is physical attraction, that is often the core of their relationship—the physical. That's how they express love.

Some people even make their decision to marry upon this basis. By itself, it may carry the marriage for three to five years, but that's it.

Eye to Eye
The second step on the ladder of a developing relationship is *eye to eye.*

‾‾| Eye to Eye
Eye to Body

It may have happened to you. You and the other person connect eye to eye at the same time. You exchange glances. For some there's a rush of embarrassment as you look away. You didn't want to be caught looking, but you were. You didn't expect to see them looking back at you, but they were. You were caught up in the words of an older song that went, "I was lookin' back to see if you were lookin' back to see if I was lookin' back at you." Then the looks continue with some subtle or obvious nonverbal expression that signals, "Let's get better acquainted." It's the feeling of looking through a keyhole and seeing another eye staring back at you. Perhaps this first happened to you in junior or senior high school. People may spend hours thinking how they're going to catch each other's eye. It's a pleasant experience.

Voice to Voice

The third step is *voice to voice*: This is the time when the initial verbal connections take place. The exchanges at this point are questions and comments that are basic, simple and exploratory. The purpose is to take the contact further than the visual evaluation to determine if there is any substance or depth to the attractive-looking "package."

> Voice to Voice
> Eye to Eye
Eye to Body

This stage can take a long time, but if the physical attraction is strong it can be accelerated. The two learn about each other's beliefs, backgrounds, opinions, pastimes, habits, opinions, likes and dislikes. If they have enough in common, a friendship develops. Sometimes that's all that develops, but in other cases it goes further. Sometimes the couple believes something more has developed, but it may not actually meet the criteria for a true friendship. Some couples rush through this stage in their haste to get connected. Some bypass it altogether. That's the first step to disaster.

Sometimes relationships that deteriorate lack the responses that occur in these initial stages. As essential as they are for the beginning of a relationship, such responses are just as important for the maintenance of the relationship.

This step is the first layer of any lasting bond that may form between a couple. If this stage can be cultivated and developed fully, a couple has a very solid base.

On the other hand, it is often at this point that a nonorganic "clinical disease" appears. It's called "infatuation," and it can happen during any of the first three stages.

≈ Infatuation could lead you to do things you might later regret. Love won't. ≈

Infatuation moves quickly; love grows. Infatuation carries a sense of uncertainty; love begins with security. Infatuation could lead you to do things you might regret; love won't. Infatuation lacks confidence—you often wonder what the other person is doing when he is not with you. Often infatuation is something only one person feels. It keeps your head in the clouds so much that it makes everything else in your life more difficult. You want the other person all to yourself. You become possessive.

Infatuation can make you a bit crazy because you live for the approval of the other person. You become more self-conscious. Infatuation leads you to dress to stimulate the other person, because his physical response reassures you that he cares for you.[1]

Infatuation, by its fickle nature, elevates or idealizes the positive traits of the other person. It opens the window shade to looking at the desirable features and pulls it down on the undesirable traits. The desirable features expand like a lump of dough filled with yeast. Soon this is all that is seen. If something undesirable comes into the picture, it is explained away.

This idealization begins to control attitudes and feelings and puts both persons on their best behavior. They're effective salespersons—whatever they do is designed to enhance their desirability. That feeds unrealistic expectations about how they'll act after marriage. Infatuation adds to the deception.

Infatuation's purpose is to propel you toward the person of

your dreams. But remember, they are just that—only in your dreams. Here is what it looks like. [2]

Objective Reality ⟶ | The Other Person | Strengths/Weaknesses

Infatuation ⟶ | The Other Person | **Strengths** (no weaknesses)
Labels: sensitive, fair, kind, considerate, generous, respectful, reasonable.

If marriage is preceded by infatuation, some serious adjustments are likely to be made, and the picture may look like this:

Disappointment ⟶ | The Other Person | **Weaknesses**
(no strengths)
Labels: insensitive, unfair, inconsiderate, selfish, rude, unreasonable.

Unfortunately, there doesn't seem to be an inoculation against the disease of infatuation. So the next best thing to help modify its impact is to understand how it develops and what it will do to your relationship.

You may think (or feel) that you will be an exception and are immune to this disease. But remember that everyone thinks this, and that the reality is—exceptions don't exist!

Dating: Pro and Con

Somewhere within these stages dating may occur. Let's really begin to meddle now. Two questions that are seldom asked should be considered: What *is* a date? *Why* do people date? Answer these for yourself. Ask some of your friends. You may be surprised at the variety of answers.

Basically a date is an agreed-upon appointment between **a** man and woman to do something together that they would both enjoy. It is assumed that during this appointment they will become better acquainted with each other for the purpose of developing a romantic relationship. As one person said, "It's a time when you go out to check out the other person."

Why do we put so much importance on dating? Our society says if you're sharp and acceptable you'll be dating. If you're not, well, there's something wrong. But who is to say that dating is the healthiest way to build a relationship? Isn't it possible for a couple to build a lasting relationship which leads to marriage without dating?

Dating can be beneficial, but it can also be detrimental to a relationship. For many couples it creates a superficial and shallow relationship. The couple is on their *best* behavior, dressed to look their *best*. They often sit passively side by side, being entertained rather than talking, and so they rarely discover who the other person is. It's actually the worst type of an environment in which to become acquainted or to evaluate a relationship.

In the book *Singles Plus*, the author suggests several reasons for dating. These include to develop friendships, to have fun, to feel good about yourself, to understand the differences between men and women, to learn to share and to get out of your shell. [3]

But couldn't all of these be accomplished without dating per se? Much of the dating process today is defective at best. For many couples what takes place during dating is intimacy but not necessarily commitment. For many, dating is a short-term, need-fulfillment process with little thought given to the possibility of permanency. Dating today is basically a relationship for sexual recreation.

Much of what occurs in dating actually hinders the development of the friendship stage of relating. Why? Because the foundation for the relationship is usually the romantic attraction rather than something more substantial. By merely agreeing to date, each participant implies to the other, "I'm interested in you romantically. Let's spend time getting to know one another." A friendship has more potential because it allows for the possibility of openly relating while spending time together pursuing common interests. If intimacy develops without friendship, there is no depth, no roots, and the potential for permanency is sabotaged.

Often two individuals who have never even met see one another, talk for a few minutes and then decide to go out on a date to "check one another out." Soon a physical relationship begins. The assumption is made that if this physical intimacy is enjoyable it must be love. Many couples have mistakenly equated love with physical involvement. Later this mistake is inevitably discovered.

Another difficulty that dating creates is that it often isolates a couple from their other relationships. I've seen this happen time and time again. One's entire focus is centered on the other person, creating a situation that can actually damage the relationship. In marriage, a spouse soon discovers that a partner cannot meet all the needs. Thus a wife has her friendships and the husband his. A balance is developed. But the exclusive nature of too many dating relationships excludes this possibility.

If you're in a relationship and you begin to focus on or just talk about the one you're dating, what does that tell you?[4]

Hand to Hand

Step four in our twelve steps to a lasting relationship is the first instance of physical contact. It's called *hand to hand*.

```
        ⌐ Hand to Hand
      ⌐ Voice to Voice
    ⌐ Eye to Eye
Eye to Body
```

Touching at this stage is usually in the context of a non-romantic situation such as the man helping the woman into the car or with a step over some obstacle. These are occasional contacts. At this point either one can back off from the relationship without this being taken as a serious rejection. If the hand-to-hand contact continues, it usually signifies the couple's romantic attachment to each other. Taking the other person's hand is making a statement—a pronouncement, as it were, that something is developing.

Arm to Shoulder
Step five is *arm to shoulder.*

```
        ┌─ Arm to Shoulder
      ┌─┘ Hand to Hand
    ┌─┘ Voice to Voice
  ──┘ Eye to Eye
Eye to Body
```

This is an affectionate embrace, but it's still noncommittal. It's almost like a "buddy" posture or position. The two are side by side and focused more on the world in front of them than they are on each other. This stage signifies that the relationship has moved closer than a close friendship, but the presence of real love is usually lacking.

Can you remember these steps? How did you feel about your partner at these stages?

Arm to Waist
The next step, stage six, finds the arm slipped downward so that the position is now *arm to waist:*

```
          ┌─ Arm to Waist
        ┌─┘ Arm to Shoulder
      ┌─┘ Hand to Hand
    ┌─┘ Voice to Voice
  ──┘ Eye to Eye
Eye to Body
```

This is a clearer indication that something romantic is occurring. The couple is now pulling their bodies closer together, but they are still looking forward. All of the previous stages are continuing, and they share more information or secrets which pertain just to them.

Some people who skip the previous steps and go directly to step six indicate that they experienced a strong romantic response and attraction the first time they saw one another. They have that

≈ If you choose to marry based on a feeling of romantic euphoria, you may soon find that if you can fall *in* love, you can fall *out* of love, too. ≈

strong, visual, heart-pounding experience which can only signify one thing—love. As one person said, "Love is a feeling you feel when you never felt that way before." The strong romantic feelings seem to override all sense and rationality. Although many choose to marry based upon this experience of euphoria, they often find that if they can fall *in* love, they can fall *out* of love, too.

Face to Face
Next a new dynamic enters the relationship. No longer is the couple just focusing on the outward world. They have moved to step seven: *face to face.*

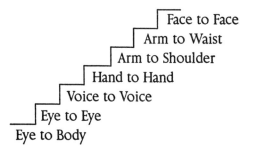

Face to Face
Arm to Waist
Arm to Shoulder
Hand to Hand
Voice to Voice
Eye to Eye
Eye to Body

Face to face is a level of contact that involves gazing into each other's eyes, hugging and kissing. If the couple progressed through the previous stages without omitting any, they have probably developed a unique communication style that enables them to connect with very few words. The new focus of attention as well as tension in the relationship is sexual desire.

Hand to Head

From here the relationship moves to the intimate stage of *hand to head.*

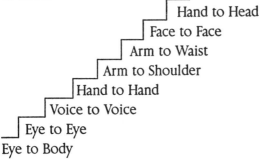

Hand to Head
Face to Face
Arm to Waist
Arm to Shoulder
Hand to Hand
Voice to Voice
Eye to Eye
Eye to Body

Hand to head is an extension of the previous stage, *face to face.* The couple will cradle or stroke each other's head while kissing or talking. It's an outward sign to others that the relationship has progressed.

This is because the head is one of the most vulnerable parts of the body. We go to great lengths to protect it, and we are careful who we allow to touch us there. It involves a great amount of trust to let another person into that area of your life.

Hand to Body

Step nine is the first of the steps involved in the ultimate knowledge of one another. It's called *hand to body.*

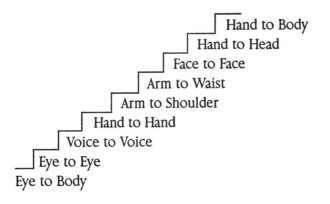

Hand to Body
Hand to Head
Face to Face
Arm to Waist
Arm to Shoulder
Hand to Hand
Voice to Voice
Eye to Eye
Eye to Body

At this stage there is more touching and caressing of other parts of the body in addition to the head. There is an appreciation and respect for the uniqueness of the body. You're aware of each other's imperfections, but can accept what is there. You like the person regardless. Some may have moved into caressing the breasts at this point, whereas others have not. The response toward each other's body may be sexual or just affectionate.

Dr. Jim Dobson tells the story of the night his father died. It's a story of deep affection at stage nine, without the sexual connotations.

> When the emergency room physician came to notify Jim's mother that her husband was gone, she asked, "May I spend some time with my husband?" The physician agreed to prepare the emergency room for her. Then, Dr. Dobson said, "My mother spent 45 minutes with my father's body. She stroked his hands, traced the outline of his feet, his face, and kissed him. She was saying good-bye to the body she had known. It was not primarily sexual, it was total knowledge that had sealed their marriage across the years."
>
> Exactly. So I suggest to lively teens that they look closely at the next group of senior citizens they encounter at a rest stop or in a restaurant. Imagine which of them is just what you will look like. Try to think why anybody would really love you after you lost your youthful body, became bald or gray, wrinkled. Some of you will suffer surgical deformity through amputation, radiation therapy or worse. What will hold your love together then? The only glue to take you through the years will be God's Creation bond that never breaks.[5]

When young couples are at this stage, affection often becomes clouded over by the sexual. This is why the last three stages of a relationship belong only to the couple and to the marriage relationship, for they are the most intimate.

The Final Stages

These final three steps are *mouth to breast, hand to genital* and *genital to genital.*

```
                                  ┌── Genital to Genital
                             ┌────┘ Hand to Genital
                        ┌────┘ Mouth to Breast
                   ┌────┘ Hand to Body
              ┌────┘ Hand to Head
         ┌────┘ Face to Face
    ┌────┘ Arm to Waist
   ┌┘ Arm to Shoulder
  ┌┘ Hand to Hand
 ┌┘ Voice to Voice
┌┘ Eye to Eye
Eye to Body
```

These final stages are the phases of sexual arousal followed by intercourse. For bonding to occur it is essential to work slowly through each stage. Intimacy is something that grows steadily and slowly.

But we have a problem today. Many couples move too fast. They don't stop at stage nine. Many couples skip stages one through eight, and *start* at nine! What chance does a lasting relationship have when there's been a bypass? It's like building a bridge over a gorge and leaving out the concrete and steel foundations. Just as the structure will be deformed, so will the relationship.[6]

Roger Hillerstrom describes this problem:

As these twelve stages illustrate, the progression is toward genital-to-genital bonding, or intercourse. The behaviors we label "petting" involve steps nine through eleven. They are preliminary to intercourse and leave no room for further progression except intercourse. A couple who wants to avoid intercourse before marriage, who does not feel ready for a marriage commitment, and yet are involved in petting, have few options open besides failure or frustration. They are attempting to pursue and intensify a natural progression, only to abort it just prior to fulfillment.

This natural progression is the force that pushes a couple who have had intercourse to continue having it—even if they feel guilty about it. This progression is also what compels a person who has had intercourse in one relationship to pursue it in the next, even when he or she knows it was a problem in the first relationship.

For most couples, petting is like shifting a car into high gear—it generally speeds up the progression towards coitus. The pursuit of physical pleasure dominates the relationship, and emotional growth and communication often come to a screeching halt.

Couples who are in the petting stage generally don't talk much, at least not in-depth. They neglect the exploration of each other's personalities in favor of exploring physical sensations. While the physical aspect escalates, the relationship stagnates. They give more and more attention and energy to being alone together and to satisfying their physical appetites. They spend less and less time being social with other people or with each other. The date becomes a time to "get through" in order to arrive at the real agenda for the evening—physical stimulation and arousal.

Before long there is very little left in the relationship besides physical involvement. Feeling close is dependent on physical contact, and giving it up feels like giving up the relationship.[7]

What are you thinking or feeling right now? Where are you in your relationship? Are you where you want to be? Are there changes you want or need to make? Think about these questions for a while. Then let's explore other aspects of a relationship in the next chapter.

Notes

1. Ray Mossholder, *Singles Plus* (Lake Mary, Fla.: Creation House, 1991), pp. 140-141. Adapted.
2. Aaron T. Beck, *Love Is Never Enough* (New York: Harper & Row, 1988), pp. 32-37. Adapted.
3. Mossholder, op. cit., pp. 67-69. Adapted.
4. Joshua Harris, *I Kissed Dating Goodbye* (Sisters, Oreg.: Multnomah Books, 1997), pp. 32-37. Adapted.
5. Dr. Donald Joy, *Bonding-Relationship in the Image of God* (Dallas, Tex.: Word Publishing, 1985), p. 51.
6. Roger Hillerstrom, *Intimate Deception* (Sisters, Oreg.: Multnomah Books, 1989), pp. 53-55. Adapted.
7. Ibid., pp. 56-57.

⑥

"It's Not a Good Sign"

≈

*It pays to recognize the signs of a healthy or an
unhealthy relationship...to know when to hang in
and work on it, and when to move on...to understand
when conflict is healthy, and when it's destructive.*

"It's not a good sign." This is a phrase you've probably heard
before. Some signs are good. Some aren't. And this applies to
relationships as well.

Perhaps you're wondering where you've been, why you've
been there in your relationships, and whether the important
indicators, or signs, are good or bad. Looking at the differences
in the following characteristics may help you understand yourself
and your partner better.

Are your various relationships healthy or unhealthy? If you
said, "Oh, they're very healthy," my question would be "How do
you know? What's the criteria?"

If you said, "Unhealthy," I'd ask the same question. How do
you know? What are you using as your criteria?

In my backyard I have two ponds and a waterfall. The water
flows from one pond down a four-foot stream into a larger pond.
An electric pump sucks in the water, sending it up a pipe and into

a stone waterfall, which cascades down into the original pond. It's repetitive. It's on a very predictable cycle.

An unhealthy relationship also follows patterns. Some men and women jump from one relationship to another and find themselves following the same pattern each time. Let's follow such a person. It could be someone you know. Many people, unfortunately, fall into this pattern.

Relating from a Position of Need

This cycle begins with a need, a feeling of emptiness. It could stem from just being alone or from feeling lonely for a while. It may result from a breakup or from just not feeling good about yourself.

Then you connect with someone and they seem to be *just* who you were looking for. You see him or her through rose-colored glasses: all pluses—no faults. You may begin to idolize this person.

But then you may begin receiving some unsolicited feedback from family and friends. "This person isn't good for you." "Watch out for them, you're going to end up hurt." "It's not the best relationship. You can do better." But you don't really hear this input. You ignore it.

You make up excuses for the relationship—excuses to defend your choice to others as well as to yourself. You have some doubts. But there are those pluses. And it's better than being alone.

Then you take the next step. You make some level of commitment to the relationship. You're tired of making excuses, so you focus on the person and distance yourself from anyone who doesn't see the relationship the way you do. Some of your convictions may drop by the wayside as well.

The relationship may continue for some time. But then your partner crosses the line in some way. He or she goes too far. It could be overcontrolling, abuse, betrayal or constant lies. You finally wake up to reality. You're upset over your entanglement and just how far you've been drawn into this relationship. Now *you*, not just your friends, are beginning to see danger signals. You even think about ending the relationship. But no, this pushes your panic button, which in turn pushes you back toward the person and overrides your feelings of concern.

This rollercoaster ride could continue for months or even years. It's an unhealthy cycle. Part of you knows it's no good and wants out. The other part says it's better than nothing. So you remain stuck.

You may or may not get to the stage of ending the relationship. You might decide to override your panic and take that step. Or the person may dump *you*. If so, you really hurt.

Then you enter a stage of withdrawal. You experience emotional as well as physical symptoms. You ache. You're lonely. How can you cope with the distress and overcome it? Simple. *You go back into the relationship.* Even if you were affirmed and supported by others for being out of the relationship, their opinion doesn't carry the weight of the relief you feel by being reconnected.

But in time this relationship ends for good. You recover from this loss, but guess what? You feel empty again. The search begins all over again, and the cycle is back in motion.

Selecting someone out of need or emptiness will cause you to settle for less than the best.

Toward Healthier Relationships

Now let's consider several possible characteristics of a healthy relationship. If you think I like lists, you're right. There are many of them in this book. Lists give us a measuring line for our lives and a clear window through which to see what we are doing. So let's consider a list that shows the difference between healthy and unhealthy relationships.

I've borrowed most of these from a friend of mine, Tom Whiteman, who shared them in a book he wrote with Randy Peterson, *Love Gone Wrong.*[1] As you consider these, evaluate your present relationship or review past ones.

1. Are you in this relationship because you clearly choose
    to be, or do you feel you "must" or "have" to be with
    that person?

Consider June. She's in a relationship and is really drawn to Tim.
She's willing to make sacrifices in order to make it work. She's giving to the relationship, but still maintains her objectivity. An
important factor is that *her judgment controls her emotions*, so
she's in charge of her choices. She expects to be treated properly
and with respect. She holds Tim accountable for his actions as he
does with her.

Sue, on the other hand, has been dating Richard for several
months. He tends to take her for granted in many ways. He is more

≈ If you freely choose to be with someone,
it's healthy. If you are driven or compelled to
be with someone, it's unhealthy. ≈

of a taker, and Sue finds herself giving more and more. The more
she gives and tries, the emptier she feels—especially because
Richard doesn't get the message that he should be a giver himself.

Although others have suggested to Sue that she could do better and needs to move on, she believes if she tries harder the
relationship will improve—and, of course, that Richard will
change. But the longer she stays in the relationship, the more she
feels controlled by it. It's as though she thinks she is making
choices. The reality is that *the relationship has taken over*. Her
freedom of choice seems to be crippled.

Which person, June or Sue, do you identify with more?

These two patterns can exist whether you're male or female.
If you freely *choose* to be with someone, it's healthy. If you are
driven or *compelled* to be with someone, it's unhealthy.

2. A healthy relationship is characterized by mutual
    strength, support and equality—you help each other
    grow, to be the best you can be.

In a healthy relationship each participant acts as a cheerleader or encourager to the other. The man and woman help each other by experiencing and expressing appropriate involvement with each other's ups and downs.

An unhealthy relationship contains a "fixer." One person takes it upon himself to reform, restructure, save, fix, or even enable the other person. The relationship is off-balance. It's tilted—and the more something tilts the greater its instability.

One person has an abundance of needs, whereas the other needs to be needed. The fixer seems to thrive on helping and being needed. Each partner attempts to save the other person from the consequences of his own choices. But this only serves to perpetuate the problem. They take action when they should let go; yet when they really should do something they fail to take the proper steps. They become caretakers, doing for the other person what that person is capable of doing for herself.

Do you know anyone like this? If so, what is their relationship like?

Dave and Jan Congo describe this person well. They say a fixer believes that:

- I am totally responsible for other people's feelings and actions.
- I am the cause of other people's problems and therefore must bail them out.
- I must meet every need and answer every cry for help.
- I am defined by the people I am in relationship with.
- I live at the mercy of other people's demands and expectations.
- I have no right to privacy, plans or personal well-being.
- I have no choice in my relationships.
- I have an insatiable need to be admired.
- I am hopelessly flawed and unchangeable.
- I am motivated by fear and guilt.
- I must save others from the negative consequences of their choices.

- I do things for people that they could and should do for themselves.
- I must never say no.[2]

You may be in a relationship like this. You may even be comfortable with it. Just remember: *When the person who needs fixing is fixed, the one who has the need to fix others isn't needed anymore.* That's one reason so many relationships and marriages fall apart. The Congos went through this adjustment and fortunately were able to turn their relationship around. This is the decision Jan says she made while at a marriage retreat:

On that fateful day at the retreat, I stopped being a dependent woman whose entire life was built around Dave. Up until then, he had been my god. I lived reacting to his needs—my life was consumed with trying to meet them. Dave was unaware of the impact his behavior was having on me. I longed to be nurtured, but when he did special things for me, I questioned and devalued everything—I even read his kindness as being manipulative. What did he want from me? Did he have an ulterior motive?

Both of us were terrified of both abandonment and engulfment. Gradually, my "underground" movement against Dave's control went from covert to overt. That's when we entered a new stage, which we now call an "isolate relationship."

At that point, I made the decision to rebuild my life around myself and my career as a college instructor. With that resolution came the birth of a two-headed monster that was to cause suffering for both of us.

During that period in our marriage we lived in isolation from each other. Instead of Dave's being the center of my world, my career became central. Dave's career had been central since we were married, so now the battle of the two-headed monster began in earnest, bringing with it distance, loneliness, lack of sensitivity, power struggles and unmet needs. I threw myself into an ever-increasing effort to define my own identity, inwardly fluctuating between anger and guilt. Meanwhile, Dave felt bewildered, threatened and betrayed. He attempted to maintain our oneness with controlling behavior. Other spouses sometimes use clinging to accomplish the same.

Although in reality we were emotionally divorced, actual divorce was not an option for us. When we got married, we had committed ourselves to each other for life. So the decision then was not whether or not we'd stay together. It was to decide what kind of life we wanted to have together. How thankful we are now that we were permanently linked for better or worse. Without that vow, we would surely have fled in the midst of the worst and would never have found out how good the best could be.[3]

There's another pattern very similar to this one. It's a pattern I've seen in many unhealthy relationships over the years. It can best be explained by something I did—and hopefully you haven't.

I once took a carton of milk out of the refrigerator, turned around to the counter, and began to pour it into a glass that I had placed there. The problem was I forgot where I had put the glass. I missed it by a foot. The milk I poured was wasted. It didn't do me any good because it was all over the counter top and dripping onto the floor. (At least my two golden retrievers appreciated it.) The milk needed to be poured into something with structure, with boundaries. It's the only way it will work.

In an unhealthy relationship, there is often a person who pours himself or herself out for their partner. One is a giver, the other a taker. But that's not the way a relationship is supposed to work. It's certainly not biblical. As we enter into any relationship, we aren't supposed to lose our individual sense of who we are. But unfortunately some people are like the glass of milk I poured all over the counter.

Do you have unhealthy boundaries? How would you know? Listed below are some of the indications. Evaluate yourself on a scale of 0 to 10 for each one. If you're currently in a relationship with someone, also evaluate where you see your partner:

1. Finding it difficult to keep confidences and secrets. 0_____10
2. Revealing too much on an intimate level too soon. 0_____10
3. Falling in love at first sight. 0_____10
4. Responding with love to anyone who shows interest in you. 0_____10
5. Thinking about the other person all the time 0_____10
6. Going against your personal standards of sexual behavior. 0_____10
7. Accepting gifts, food or touching that you don't want. 0_____10
8. Believing that your opinion doesn't matter. 0_____10
9. Wearing yourself out "doing" for another (especially when the other doesn't reciprocate). 0_____10
10. Letting others make decisions for you. 0_____10
11. Letting others dictate to you how you feel. 0_____10
12. Letting a partner make the decision on who your friends will be. 0_____10
13. Tolerating any kind of abuse whether emotional, physical or sexual. 0_____10
14. Feeling obligated to do things for others you barely know. 0_____10
15. Having a difficult time saying no, even when you know you should; when you do, you feel guilty. 0_____10

How do you see yourself now? Are you satisfied with where you are? What about your partner? What did you learn about this person from this exercise?

3.   Being objective about each other as compared to wearing blinders.
If your relationship is healthy, you will recognize strengths and

faults in both yourself and your partner. You will be able to see shortcomings and areas in which you need to grow.

Believe it or not, there are relationships in which the "love is blind" statement is true. One sees the other almost as a demigod. They can do no wrong. Faults are nonexistent because they are denied or overlooked.

If the other person is perfect, what happens to the need for growth? This isn't love, it's infatuation—a giant balloon which blinds us from seeing who the other person really is. One day it bursts and you're shocked by what you see.

Honesty must be an ingredient in your relationship; however, there are distinct differences between honesty and criticism. Honesty is sharing truth and feelings in a straightforward fashion, in a way that indicates fairness and respect. It means being frank, but with tact and sensitivity.

≈ When a relationship becomes an imprisonment, eventually there'll be a jailbreak! ≈

Criticism, however, means you make judgments, find faults, censor opinions and show disapproval because others don't respond or say things in the way you want. It's saying, "My way is the best and *only* way to do something; if you don't, you're wrong and deficient."

Look at the following differences between honesty and criticism. Is this what you've experienced? This list was put together by the authors of *Two Friends in Love*.

Honesty can hurt, but criticism always injures.
Honesty brings healing, but criticism promotes pain.
Honesty is shared with open hands; criticism contains a
    pointing, accusing finger.
Honesty is straightforward; criticism involves game-playing.
Honesty wants the good for both of you whereas criticism
    wants good for the critic.

Honesty is built on facts and principles; criticism builds on assumptions and unrealistic assumptions.
Honesty is unselfish; criticism wants only what it wants.
With honesty, you both win. With criticism, you both lose.[4]

4.   A fourth area of concern deals with balance between other friends and exclusive attention to your partner.
Do you have freedom or confinement in your relationship?

Some who develop a meaningful relationship with another person add the person to their life and continue relationships with friends and involvement in other activities. As feelings for the significant other increase, both parties want to spend more time with each other and less with others.

This is normal and natural. Close relationships will tend to alter schedules to some extent. In a healthy relationship, you know you have priority in each other's lives. But you don't live exclusively for each other. Some of your needs are met by others outside the relationship. If your relationship is healthy, longtime friendships won't be a threat.

But when all your time and attention is eaten up by the other person, you'll end up feeling confined and controlled. Your romantic interest cannot meet all of your needs, no matter how hard you try. Friends may continue to meet your recreational, social and intellectual needs. A relationship is not meant to be an imprisonment, either self-imposed or other-imposed. If it becomes an imprisonment, eventually there'll be a jailbreak!

5.   Healthy relationships have a high degree of trust.
You believe in the other person to do the right thing. You take him at his word. You give her the benefit of the doubt. You don't make assumptions about your partner in a negative direction. If you do make any assumptions, they're in a positive direction.

But if there's jealousy—well, listen to this description:

Jealousy is an ugly monster. It can take over a relationship and destroy it. Jealousy is born of insecurity and desire. It is not known to be reasonable. Wild charges are made, exposing deep feelings of pain or fear. If you have been jealous within a relationship, you know how it gnaws at you, defying your attempts to control it. If your partner has been the jealous one, you know how frustrating it can be to sidestep the traps that monster sets.

The jealous person fears that the partner will leave for someone more physically attractive, more interesting, more suitable, or more financially stable. This possibility creates panic and results in irrational attempts to control the partner's life. This reaction can chase the partner away unless the partner is addicted, too.[5]

If trust isn't there at the start of a relationship, how can it ever develop? Relationships usually start out trusting because you don't have a history of hurt. Possessiveness is dangerous. It pushes away the person you're attempting to keep.

To what degree do you tend to be a trusting person?

To what degree does your partner tend to be a trusting person?

To what degree do you tend to be a jealous person?

To what degree does your partner tend to be a jealous person?

A healthy relationship contains two individuals (not just one) who are open to change, rather than clinging to unhealthy patterns from their past.

6. **Those who are open to change have more opportunity to operate or function as they should.**

"Functional" and "dysfunctional" are popular terms today. The authors of *Love Gone Wrong* give a good example of the difference:

When I'm driving my car, I have a problem if I have a flat tire. I might even consider it a crisis. And I could probably call it a *misfunction*. The tire, being flat, isn't doing what a tire should. I stop and fix it and drive on.

But if my car is badly out of alignment, that's another thing. It affects my steering, the car wobbles to the right as I drive, and my tires get worn quickly on one side, leading to more flat tires. It might be considered a *dysfunction*. It's not just when one thing goes wrong. It's when the whole system goes out of whack.[6]

In an earlier chapter, we talked about your past. How are your past and your partner's past impacting your relationship? Are each of you moving ahead or repeating patterns? Do you see yourselves responding to others in the same way you did 10 years ago, or are you changing?

The word *change* means to make different, to give a different course or direction, to replace one thing with another, to make a shift from one to another, to undergo transformation, transition or substitution. However, to most people change is negative, something that implies inferiority, inadequacy and failure. No wonder so many people resist the idea of change. Who wants to feel inferior and inadequate?

The Bible has a lot to say about growth, change and becoming mature. While God loves us just the way we are, He loves us too much to leave us that way. Because He loves us, He wants to see us "become conformed to the image of His Son" (Rom. 8:29, *NASB*). Because He loves us, He wants to help us "grow up in all aspects into Him, who is the head, even Christ" (Eph. 4:15, *NASB*).

In 1 Corinthians 3:1 Paul expressed concern over the Corinthian Christians because they hadn't grown. "And I, brethren, could not speak to you as to spiritual men, but as to men of flesh, as to babes in Christ" (*NASB*).

The writer of Hebrews also expressed concern that his readers hadn't changed. They hadn't deepened or matured (see Heb. 5:11-14). The author exhorted them to "press on to maturity" (Heb. 6:1, *NASB*). What he was really saying was, "Hey, folks, it's time for you to make some changes. It's time for you to grow up."

Our willingness to change, to learn, to grow is God's love language. It tells Him we believe in Him, we trust Him, we want to be who and what He wants us to be. Openness to change is our way of taking His hand and following Him. He will never give us more than we can handle (see 1 Cor. 10:13). He can cause all things to work together for good (see Rom. 8:28). And He will supply all of our needs according to His riches in glory (see Phil. 4:19).

How do we grow up? How do we mature? How do we become who God wants us to be? How do we learn to honor one another, to serve one another, to prefer others as more important than ourselves?

In 1 Peter 1:7 Peter uses a powerful word picture to describe this process. He compares our lives to gold that is purified by fire. The refining process involves several different "finings" to bring the alloys and impurities to the surface so that the goldsmith can remove them. The refining process takes time and hard work. At times it can be painful. But the product is worth it. The end result is pure gold.

Warren Wiersbe says:

> We can benefit from change. Anyone who has ever really lived knows that there is no life without growth. When we stop growing we stop living and start existing. But there is no growth without change, there is no challenge without change. Life is a series of changes that create challenges, and if we are going to make it, we have to grow.[7]

But to change you have to be a risk-taker. To have a relationship you have to be a risk-taker.

When you take a risk, you open your hand and loosen your hold on what is certain. You reach out for something that is a bit uncertain, but usually better than what you have at the present time. Tim Hansel, who is certainly a risk-taker, writes:

> Have you ever thought what your life would be like if you had never taken a risk? You probably would have never learned to walk, never moved away from home, never made a friend, and never really gone anywhere or done

anything the least bit memorable. The truth is, we cannot grow without taking risks, without loosening our grip on the known and the certain, and taking a chance in reaching for a little bit more of life. Some people are content with mere routine, a revolving-door existence of waking up, eating breakfast, going to work, coming home, going to bed. But others seem infected with a rage to live. Their secret is that they are always beginning something new![8]

≈ To change and grow, you have to risk. To move ahead, you have to risk. To find what is worthwhile in life, you have to risk. ≈

To change and grow, you have to risk. To move ahead, you have to risk. To find what is worthwhile in life, you have to risk. To risk means giving up some security (though some of what we call security is really false, since it doesn't really give us what we think it does).

There is a 25-mile stretch of highway in the high desert area of Southern California that I travel once or twice a year. It's not my favorite stretch of road because of the limitation of the two lanes and the frequent dips in the road that tend to hide oncoming cars. When I'm stuck behind a slow-plodding driver, I have the choice of staying behind him or looking for an opportunity to pass. When I think about passing, I must not only observe the slow vehicle I'm following but watch the road for oncoming traffic. Then I have to determine if there is enough highway between me and the approaching cars to allow me to pass.

These are the stages involved: preparing adequately, making a commitment, then following through by pressing the accelerator to the floor, surging around the slow driver and moving back into the right lane. This process is successful for most people when they follow all the procedures. But it doesn't work for the driver who hesitates and vacillates when he pulls out into the left lane. Losing his nerve and not accelerating properly can lead to a tragic accident.

Similarly, when we risk and choose to change in the area of personal growth, we must be committed to follow through. I would rather *choose* to take a risk than be forced into taking one. Which would you prefer? If we postpone taking risks when they are needed, we may be forced to accept something we don't want, or to take risks when we are least prepared for them.

What needs to be changed at this time in your life?

Howard Hughes, one of the richest men of the twentieth century, is a good example of what can happen when we risk—and when we refuse to take risks. Hughes greatly impacted the aircraft industry with bold risks for change, helping the United States maintain dominance in the sky during several wars. He also helped establish the movie industry and influenced the entire entertainment industry. He gained tremendous power, which affected not only our society but the world.

Howard Hughes was a pioneer at risk-taking for a large part of his life. But then he changed. He redirected his energies to becoming a fanatic at protecting himself against risk. He created a virtual prison for himself in his attempt to insulate himself from decisions, people, germs or anything else he perceived to be a risk. He was worth billions, but he chose to live in a hotel room and vegetate until he died. He ended up a fearful old man who didn't trust anyone—a prisoner when he could have been free. When Howard Hughes stopped risking he stopped living.[9]

Remember: In unhealthy relationships people bind themselves to the past and refuse to change and grow.

7. A healthy relationship moves conflicts toward resolution, and uses disagreement as a means of growth.

No relationship is totally without conflict. In healthy relationships, the partners are determined to resolve conflicts, to make each conflict a means of growth. Unhealthy relationships often develop into love-hate relationships. Think about this.

Some people seem to thrive on volatile relationships. But the crucial question is, Where is the relationship going? Are the two people growing together with each new disagreement? Or are they just replaying the same old issues? How do the partners handle conflict? Are they resolving it through healthy give-and-take? Or are they at an impasse, with neither one giving in? When they do get back together, is it because they've decided to make the necessary compromises to work out their problem? Or do they just "need" each other so much that they decide to ignore the problem until it flares up again?

Every relationship has its disagreements. But in a healthy relationship, the partners talk through the problems, work through them, learn through them, learn about each other, learn about themselves and move on. That's growth. That may mean the relationship reaches a higher level of understanding and commitment. Or that may mean the partners decide the romantic relationship isn't worth pursuing. Either way, the individuals grow as they deal with their conflicts.[10]

Some relationships just move from one unresolved conflict to another. I've seen couples in marital counseling who come in and say, "It's not that we don't talk about our issues. We've been talking about them for 20 years. We just don't resolve them." They have never learned the necessary problem-solving skills.

Many unhealthy relationships are characterized by avoidance. They don't talk about the issues, but bury them. In time, however, the hot issues smolder and eventually create a blowup that could last for days. Then once again there's calm. It's a repetitive cycle.

Remember that conflict is simply a difference in point of view. Many conflicts are unconscious ways of adjusting the distance between partners. People fight both when they want distance and when they want closeness.

Conflict can accomplish several things. It leads to a discovery of truth. It stretches our perspective, enabling us to consider more than one point of view. It helps us change our patterns of communication. We learn what works and what doesn't. It opens up blocked lines of communication. Then we can become solution-oriented instead of problem-oriented. We learn to search out solutions together rather than trying to change the other person.[11]

8. **Finally, a healthy relationship makes you a stronger person, both when you're with your partner and when you're not.**

In a good relationship, you feel good about yourself and the relationship the day after you've been together, even though you've had an argument. In an unhealthy relationship you may experience a high when you're together, but a major letdown when you're apart. Even if you need to end the relationship, you are left without the strength that you need to take such a step.[12]

If you see issues and problems in your relationship based on this chapter, there are some steps you can take. Relationships aren't always easy, especially if they're unhealthy. They may take more work than you expect.

The first thing you can do is define what you want and what you need from your relationship. Be specific and describe it in writing. Then identify precisely what you are willing to give to the relationship. If you have a trusted group of close friends or an older mentor-type couple, discuss this with them and gain their feedback.

Then spend time talking with your partner. First ask her what she wants and needs from the relationship. Give her advance warning that you want to discuss this. You're more likely to get information this way. Then share with her what you want or need.

This may sound structured or contrived, and one or both of you may resist doing this. But consider this: Is what you're doing now working? If not, why keep doing it? There's got to be a better way!

Some couples have discovered that it helps to create an agreed-upon set of rules and guidelines. You will need to agree on the terms of your relationship. That could include the amount of time you spend together, as well as time with friends; who does what for whom; no critical comments in public; not assuming that you have a date, but always asking; calling if you're running late; not asking for inappropriate favors. You may want to set a time limit as to when you must see changes.

If you agree on these guidelines and the other person violates them, you could give her another chance; but it would appear that the handwriting is already on the wall. If there's another violation, take action. Move on—no matter how the other person begs or pleads. Yes, it may be painful, but the pain of going on is worse.[13] You have a decision to make.

Notes

1. Thomas A. Whiteman and Randy Peterson, *Love Gone Wrong* (Nashville: Thomas Nelson, 1994), pp. 54-56. Adapted.
2. Dave and Jan Congo, *The Power of Love* (Chicago: Moody Press, 1993), p. 34.
3. Ibid., pp. 57-58.
4. Ed and Carol Newenschwander, *Two Friends in Love* (Sisters, Oreg.: Multnomah Books, 1986), pp. 154-155. Adapted.
5. Whiteman and Peterson, op. cit., p. 46.
6. Ibid., pp. 49-50.
7. From a message by Warren Wiersbe on the "Back to the Bible" broadcast.
8. Tim Hansel, *Holy Sweat* (Dallas, Tex.: Word Publishing, 1987), p. 4.
9. David Viscott, *Risking* (New York: Pocket Books, 1977), pp. 18-21, 28. Adapted.
10. Whiteman and Peterson, op. cit., p. 52.
11. Congo, op. cit., p. 70. Adapted.
12. Whiteman and Peterson, op. cit., pp. 34-36. Adapted.
13. Ibid., p. 174. Adapted.

What's the Relationship Potential?

≈

*Let's face it: Not every relationship you think at first
will work into something long-term really should...
or could. What are some ways you can tell?*

Have you ever heard of the phrase "relationship potential"? It's a
way of assessing whether you're riding a live horse or a dead one.
In other words, it's a way of determining whether or not you and
your partner have a realistic hope for a future together.

All relationships have a future—either together or apart. Most
couples who begin a relationship, whether it's talked about or
not, hope there is a positive future for them. But after months
and years of invested time, many don't. It's possible to save time,
energy and a lot of heartache if you engage in a preliminary
screening process.

When a company is selecting someone to fill a very important
position, they screen a number of candidates. Many are elimi-
nated during this initial step. Wouldn't you be wise to do something similar regarding a possible close relationship? There are
probably a number of people you would never spend more than

a few weeks with, or even a few days, if you knew who they really were. Their mismatch potential is tremendous. Let's consider that potential in this chapter.

There will be exceptions to every concern mentioned. And most people want to think of themselves as the exception rather than the rule. Don't! Think of yourself as the rule—then if you end up being the exception you'll be delighted.

Out of Balance

One of the relationships that has a low potential is the "out of balance" relationship. This is one where you care more for the other person than that person cares about you. Or he cares more about you than you do for him. Either way, the relationship is out of balance. It's tilting. One may be pursuing while the other wants to pull back.

Sometimes the one who is not as invested in the relationship actually works at trying to become more interested, to develop his or her love response, believing that feelings of love will develop over time.

You may think that this contrast in how you respond to each other simply indicates differences in your personalities. Perhaps, but it may also be a lack of interest or caring.

It's difficult to admit that you may care more for the other person than he or she does for you. When you think about it, you get a sinking feeling in the pit of your stomach. And then you may rationalize yourself out of accepting the facts, or you may move into a state of denial.

I've seen the shock on husbands' and wives' faces in marriage counseling when they discover their spouse's commitment level to their marriage is totally different than what they thought it was. And what is sad is that some of these marriages existed (there is no other word to describe it—just existing!) this way for decades.

What are some indications that your relationship is a mismatch—that you have a higher level of interest in the relationship than your significant other?

- You initiate most of the contact in the relationship.
- You initiate most of the affectionate advances, such as holding hands, hugging, kissing, etc.
- You are the plan maker, whereas the other just seems to go along.
- You sacrifice to do things for the other or make life more agreeable, but you don't see this reciprocated.
- You are excited about the relationship, while the other person just seems to be along for the ride.
- You talk about your relationship and possible future plans, but this strikes an unresponsive chord with your partner.

Could this be just a difference in your personalities? Possibly. But if so, then you can expect the person to be this way the rest of your life. Is this what you want? Can you live this way? Whether it's a personality difference or the other person really doesn't care as much, either way there's trouble on the horizon for this relationship!

Rescuer or the Rescued?
When I was in high school and college, some of my friends had summer jobs as lifeguards on the beaches and public pools. To me, lifeguarding was a dream job. These guys were in the sun all day, usually surrounded by kids their own age. The hours were good and the scenery was great! As summer came to an end, I'd say to them, "What a great summer job you had! I'll bet you're sorry it's over."

Many of them surprised me by saying, "Not really. I'm glad to be getting back to school. I'm tired of constantly rescuing people."

When it comes to relationships, some people never tire of being a rescuer. They live for it. But there's a problem with that. A relationship is not going to work if either one of you habitually rescues the other.

In a healthy relationship, you want to be there for the other person and he wants to be there for you. That's the healthy way to relate. But if you find you're the one who is always there for your partner, and he's like a ghost when you need him, you've got a problem.

Sometimes you may be the one who takes the initiative to rescue. Or your partner insists that you rescue him, either by solving his problem or protecting him from the consequences of his own behavior.

When you rescue your partner on a continual basis, you're teaching that individual that there's no need for him to change since you will bail him out. He won't learn from past blunders, either. Also, if you rescue him so regularly that others are aware of it, their reinforcing comments will tend to keep you locked into that pattern of behavior.

If you rescue others, what do you expect from them? Thanks, appreciation, perhaps even reciprocation. But in a close relationship you will often find this response lacking—especially if your partner is a taker. This is because when you rescue others you are exerting some type of control over them; and in time they can end up resenting you for it. The unspoken, subtle message conveyed to them is, "I'm better than you are, and you're not capable of handling things yourself."

I've seen rescuers repeat this pattern with different partners. They seemed to be attracted to people who need them. If you find that this is the case with you, what is the future for this relationship? And what is this saying about you? Are you choosing a partner for his strengths or weaknesses? Can you respond in a healthy way to a strong partner? If not, you have some work to do to discover and eliminate the needs you have to be a rescuer.[1]

But They Have Such Great Potential!
Another relationship with low potential is one in which your partner is not what you want him to be, or what you had hoped for, yet you find yourself thinking, *But they have such great potential!*

Perhaps he's not what you're looking for spiritually. But you think, *The Lord could really do wonders with him!*

Perhaps his ambition and drive to get ahead is a bit lacking. That's an understatement. *But he's just waiting for the right opportunity to come along.*

Perhaps your partner's emotional outbursts are a bit much for you. *But I'll be able to help him get a handle on that anger and depression eventually.* It doesn't matter that his friends tell you that the mood swings have always been there and are getting more intense as the years go by. Look out!

Perhaps the way your partner eyes the opposite sex is just because you're not committed or married yet. *But once that happens, he'll only have eyes for me and no one else.* Are you serious?!

≈ You can try to reshape, remake and reconstruct your partner, but you can't get gold out of a mine that's filled with lead. ≈

Perhaps the way he handles his finances is a bit scary, especially with all those credit cards maxed out. But you think, *I'm sure he'll learn responsibility once we're married.* In fact, didn't he offer to open a joint checking account and credit card with you so the two of you could learn to work closer together financially? That will be a real learning experience for you—like The Road to Bankruptcy 101! Do you really expect marriage to create a miracle?

Perhaps he doesn't communicate very much or share with you on an emotional level. But you rationalize, *Who would coming out of that abusive, alcoholic, dysfunctional background?* You've met his parents and they're both cases out of a mental health textbook. In time you expect to fill in all those gaps for your partner and he'll become a whole person. Of course, there may be nothing left of you, either!

Perhaps the reason he has jumped from relationship to relationship is that no one has ever really cared for him enough, been truly accepting of him or encouraged him to grow spiritually. *Getting him involved in my church and Bible study should make a difference.* Do you really want to do that to those people at church?

If you believe all of these possibilities, then the problem is not the other person. You know who it is.

First of all, you can't reshape, remake and reconstruct another person to this degree. You can't get gold out of a mine that's filled with lead. I've seen people in marriages like this. They end up frustrated, critical and feeling betrayed and hopelessly trapped. They would plead, beg, shout and threaten their partner, but all to no avail.

Why would anyone fool themselves to this degree? There are reasons. Some people feel called to be reformers. They like to reshape others, or at least try to. In doing so they ease the pain of looking at some of the issues of their own life.

The Perfectionistic Partner
Controllers and perfectionists are others who will embark on a crusade to "help others fulfill their potential." This is another type of relationship that has low potential—when one person is full of anger and controlling tendencies, or is a practicing perfectionist. Many of them stay married, but the unpleasantness quotient is quite high.

Let's consider perfectionism. This was mentioned earlier in the book. The very word "perfectionist" strikes fear in the heart of the person who dates or lives with one. But for perfectionist partners, the word brings a sense of satisfaction, security, their calling in life. It's an elusive calling—I have yet to meet a successful perfectionist.

Most of us would like to be successful. Some of us, however, turn success into a requirement. When this happens, we become preoccupied with the pursuit, not of excellence, but of perfection. The greater the degree of pursuit, the more often our joy is lessened. Perfectionism becomes a mental monster.

Not all perfectionists are pure perfectionists. Some of us are merely "pocket" perfectionists, singling out only a few pockets or areas of our lives that we want to be perfect. And there are times when we may want someone who is helping us to be a perfectionist. If I'm having brain surgery, I'd certainly like my surgeon to be a perfectionist, or at least the best one available!

In order to prove they are good enough, perfectionists strive to do the impossible. They set unrealistic goals and sky-high standards for a relationship. They see no reason why they should not achieve them. They strain to reach these goals, and they expect their spouses to live up to them as well. They're driven by "musts," "shoulds," "have-tos" and "never-good-enoughs." They overschedule, overwork, overdo and come unglued when there are surprises or unforeseen changes. Soon they are overwhelmed by the arduous task they have set for themselves.

The standards of a thoroughgoing perfectionist are so high that no one could consistently attain them. They are beyond reach and reason. The strain of reaching is continual, but the goals are impossible. Yet perfectionists believe their worth is determined by attaining these goals.

Because perfectionists live with the fear of failure, they often procrastinate. They take positive traits to the extreme and make them liabilities. Neatness, punctuality, responsibility and attention to details are usually assets; but a perfectionist contaminates them.

Perfectionists may also have difficulty with anger. After all, when you and others can't meet the absolute standards, frustration arises.

Perfectionism is not so much a type of behavior as it is an attitude or a belief. One belief is that *mediocrity breeds contempt.* The thought of being ordinary is intolerable. Even the garden planted or the lunch served must be the best. The person they date must also be perfect in every possible way. Perfectionists have to have the best grammar and speech, the best-behaved children, the best communication, the best dishes. The standards they set for others are unbearable. They frequently cause others to give up. The perfectionist is not really competing with other people, but reacting to the inner message, *You can do better.*

Often the perfectionist lives by extremes, to do *all or noth-*

ing. "Either I go on a diet all the way or not at all." They make you follow this pattern as well.

Another perfectionist belief is the importance of *going it alone.* It is a sign of weakness to delegate or ask for assistance, so the perfectionist must not ask for advice or opinions. This does little to promote intimacy in a relationship. You as the partner end up feeling isolated.

Perfectionists think there is *one correct way to complete a task.* Their main job is to discover that one right way. So again, until they have made that discovery, they may hesitate to begin. "Why make the wrong choice?" This even keeps some people from committing themselves in marriage, for they certainly do not want to make the wrong selection.

A perfectionist man or woman has great trouble finding an acceptable marriage partner. Perfectionists want perfect mates, not human ones. Sometimes they reject potential partners, often delaying marriage for years. They have difficulty forming relationships close enough to lead to marriage.

One man in his early 40s told me he had dated hundreds of women looking for the perfect one. He is still single today. Some people simply give up the attempt to form close human ties and devote themselves to work, not realizing that it lies within their power to change their attitude toward themselves. Such is the case with many otherwise successful bachelors and career women.

A perfectionist often looks upon marriage as another achievement. A prospective mate may at first be viewed through rose-colored glasses and seen as "perfect." But the fantasy soon fades, especially after marriage. A friend of mine, Dr. Dave Stoop, describes the situation graphically when he said, "The spouse is no longer a prince or princess, but has turned into a project!" Now the focus of attention is on making the imperfect partner perfect!

When they do marry, perfectionists don't know how to enjoy themselves. They generally continue their perfectionist attitudes, demanding perfect order in their own lives as well as the lives of others. A woman becomes anxious if the house is not in order at all times, with eggs done to a split-second three minutes, toast to a precise shade of tan, clothes hung a certain way, and perfect children from her perfect husband. What a grind!

I've seen married men and women who don't allow their partners to get to know them. They tend to retreat and live behind closed emotional doors. They're afraid they'll be found lacking in some way. Many a husband quietly accepts his perfectionistic wife's demands that he not wear shoes in the living room because she is afraid he'll leave scuffs on her "perfect" carpet. Oh, he puts up with this; but not only does he not feel comfortable in his own home, in time his feelings for his wife change.

Perfectionists have a "corrector" tendency. There is a right and perfect way to do everything, and it's according to their gospel. When you're washing the dishes, they walk over and turn down the water because you're using too much. They rearrange the canned goods in your cupboard according to their system of efficiency. They make unsolicited comments about your choice of ties and shirts or dresses with comments like, "I just want you to look your best and make a good impression." They follow you around the house turning out the lights even when you've just stepped out of the room for a few seconds. And then you hear continuously, "We're wasting money."

When you're married to a perfectionist it's easy to fall into the trap of blaming and berating yourself, walking on eggshells, getting down on yourself when your overly sensitive partner is offended by your constructive criticism, or resenting your spouse's continual intrusiveness into your life.[2] Keep in mind that perfectionism is neither a spiritual gift nor a calling from the Lord. It's the way certain personalities choose to build their own security.

The Controller
Perhaps your partner isn't a perfectionist but just a controlling type of person. You will probably feel the same pressure with this type of person as you would with a perfectionist.

Men and women use control to protect themselves from real or imagined concerns. Their use of control is part of their survival system. They believe that "the best defense is an offense"—the offensive strategy of staying in control. They live in fear of the results and consequences of not being in control. They're afraid of rejection, abandonment, hurt, disappointment and losing control itself. They may also be addicted to the respect, power or emotional rush they get from controlling others. Is this any one you know?

I've worked with numerous controllers in counseling. Their controlling tendency is an integral part of their personality. Some have even said, "I know I control. But why not? I have a lot to offer and I know what I'm talking about. Why waste time? I want to see things happen—fast and efficiently. And I can do that!" That's sad. It can destroy people as well as relationships.

Controllers use a variety of methods to get you to do what they want. One response is emotional indebtedness. Their message is, "You owe me," and this pushes your guilt button.

"If it weren't for the good words I put in for you with my friend, you never would have had that opportunity."

"Meeting me has really salvaged your life."

Sarcasm is a favorite response with controllers. You feel its bite. And often the tone and nonverbals (which make up 93 percent of the message in face-to-face conversation) are the means intended to control you.

Consider a statement like, "Oh, sure, you remembered that we're going out to dinner tonight. Then how come you arrived here an hour late looking like you've been cleaning out the garage? Sure you remembered." This emotional hook not only drags you in, but you can feel the irritation beginning to build. Your stomach churns and your pulse quickens. The more you explain, the worse it gets. The accuser's sarcasm and disbelief just increase. It is irritating to be labeled a liar.

One of the hooks of a controller is an *assumed agreement* with an underlying threat of criticism. "Sue, now stop and think about this for a minute. Then you'll see I'm right, and it's best to go along with this. Any intelligent adult could see this right away." You end up feeling trapped.

Another hook makes you the victim of a *forced choice*. "Jim, tell me which day you can clean the garage. I'd like to know now. Not tomorrow, but right now." You feel the pressure beginning to build. Later you probably feel anger toward your spouse, but also at yourself for getting pulled into the trap.

In another clever method, the controller *pretends to be talking about himself while making it clear he's talking about you.* He says such things as, "I should have known better. Letting you use that equipment was a mistake. It's my fault for letting you use it, and now it's ruined."

Or have you ever heard something like this? "You really shouldn't let your parents run your life like that, you know. At 38 years old, you need to be your own person. When are you going to break loose from their control? Maybe that's why you're not married yet." This is a *judgment* statement, and it's designed to inform you that the controller knows what's best for your life.

Every now and then I read or hear a disclaimer made by an organization or television station: "The views expressed by this speaker are not necessarily the views of the management of this station." I've heard controllers voice similar *disclaimers*. They say, "I don't mean to be critical but...," or "I don't mean to be telling you how to run your life, but...." Oh, but they *do* want to run your life! They know it, and you know it, but you don't know what to do about it.

Sometimes a controller's criticism is hidden so deeply in a statement it's difficult to confront it directly. *Imbedded* or *implied* criticism is like that. Often it's expressed in the form of a question, but it's not just a question. The hook is in the delivery. There's usually a surprised or amazed tone of voice. "You aren't actually going to wear that to this fancy party are you?" The message is, the controller doesn't like it and you should know better.

Both controllers and perfectionists use absolutes such as *always* and *never*. They fail to give you the benefit of the doubt. You may have heard phrases like, "If it weren't for you...," or "Because of you I...." These are *blame and shame* statements. Responsibility for whatever has gone wrong in the controller's life is thrust onto your shoulders, whether valid or not. And the more defensive you become, the greater the level of the controller's deafness.

Controllers are clever. They often *shift the blame* to get their point across. This way they don't have to shoulder responsibility. "It doesn't bother me that you're not going to attend, but I think it is going to bother your parents. You know how they are!" Controllers just can't seem to come out and be straight and truthful. When you try to confront them by saying, "Are you saying *you're* bothered too?" they will deny it forever.

I've heard wives use this approach with their husbands. "Some wives would be upset if their husbands took the entire weekend off to go fishing," they say. Then when their husbands ask if they would be offended they quickly respond, "Oh, no. Not me. But some wives I know would be."

Double-implied messages are characteristic of controllers. Their message contains denial of what they're saying, but you know it's still true. "Oh, go on. Why should I mind that you can't call your old mother every day?"[3]

You may be thinking, *I know a number of relationships and marriages where one of them is a perfectionist or a controller. They're still together. It's working for them!* But is it? Staying together is not the same as a relationship in which both individuals have the freedom to grow, to be all that God wants them to be, and to be comfortable with one another. If perfectionists and/or controllers can learn to give up these false bases for security, then growth can occur. I've seen this take place. But the work needs to begin before marriage.

The Pedestal Predicament

Putting your partner on a pedestal and seeing him as a "great catch" also lowers the "relationship potential." If the person you are interested in lost his position in his company, his fame or whatever unique ability that sets him apart, would you still be interested in him? Or if *you* lost these factors, would your partner still be interested in you?

I remember a woman who was telling me about the man she was becoming serious with, and as she listed all of his various attributes she mentioned he earned over $100,000 a year. I simply asked her how she would feel about him if he only earned $20,000 a year. She looked a bit shocked when I said this, then hesitantly said, "Well...I don't know. I'd never thought about it...."

I asked, "What would it mean if he didn't make that? Could he still take you where he does, dress the same, drive that sports car? What about it?" She had to think about that for a while.

≈ A relationship is made up of two individuals contributing their unique gifts and strengths. Each of you contributes to the other. If the giving is one-sided, it won't work. ≈

Unfortunately, some people use relationships or even marriage to move up in the world. If you are in this type of relationship, there are numerous factors to keep in mind. You could be giving that other person more influence, power or control over you than you should. Are you bragging about this individual to impress others and elevate your status in their eyes? You may be elevating him or her so much that you consider yourself less than you are. You need to see your own value and strengths. A relationship is made up of two individuals contributing their unique gifts and strengths. Each of you contributes to the other. If it's one-sided, it won't work.

Anger: Will It Draw You Closer, Or...?

Another potential relationship problem is when one or both of you are habitually angry. I don't mean the occasional normal angry response that we all experience. I mean when one's life reflects a continual pattern of irritation—which, by the way, is anger. Relationships will bring out this tendency. A relationship can even be a factory for the production of anger.

If you or the person you're interested in is characterized by anger, be cautious. Scripture itself cautions us in strong words:

> Make no friendships with a man given to anger, and with a wrathful man do not associate, lest you learn his ways and get yourself into a snare (Prov. 22:24,25, *Amp.*).

The wording here—*ish hemot*, or "man of heats"—literally refers to a hothead, a person who flares up at the drop of a hat.

Some men and women express anger like a heat-seeking missile. Often there are no alarms, no warning. Others express it subtly, like a snake gliding silently through the underbrush. But it still strikes you just the same.

Anger can wear many faces, but when you live with it your love soon wears thin. Anger is necessary, for its energy prompts us to take positive action. But anger can also wear an ugly face— especially in a relationship. Remember that anger has the potential of robbing you of the joy of life since it affects every aspect of your personal and relational life.

Turn anger too much inward and it destroys you. Turn it outward too much and it destroys others. Sure, expressing your anger can be a relief; but like many other things it has a price tag. The cost could be a strained relationship, a tension-filled relationship or emotional distance.

Anger carelessly expressed will override the love, care and appreciation that create close relationships. An angry person is not pleasant. Anger erects barriers. It leads to aggression, rather than reducing it.

Some people don't just express anger, they rage. Such anger can turn into hostility and bitterness. These are sudden surges of emotion that occur when you hold on to anger with an attitude of resentment. It's an attitude you develop toward life as well as toward people.

Do you know the background of the word "hostile"? It's from

a Latin word that means "enemy." It implies overt antagonism, an unfriendly and inhospitable spirit. And the more the feeling is fed the more it grows.

Let me give you a worst-case scenario for anger. You're driving on the freeway. Less than six feet away, traveling in the opposite direction, vehicles are passing you at 65 miles an hour. Sometimes the wind from their speed shakes your car a bit, more so when a semitrailer flies by. You aren't bothered by these vehicles streaking by, however, as you continue to your destination. Why should you be? You're safe—as long as you stay in your lane and they stay in theirs.

All our highways are set up in this manner. Vehicles in one lane roar in one direction, and those on the other side zip in the opposite direction. A crucial center line divides the two lanes. You are completely safe—that is, until someone crosses the line. And then you're dead.

It happens every day. Someone falls asleep, doesn't pay attention, loses control, drives under the influence, or blows a tire. The vehicle crosses the line right in front of an innocent driver. Both cars are destroyed, along with their occupants. That's what happens when the line is crossed. It's a violation with disastrous results.

When anger crosses the line of intensity and appropriate expression and becomes abusive, this, too, is a violation—with lasting results. Most people in relationships never give such expressions of anger a thought. If they do, it's to think that it happens to others, never to them.

Let's think again. It's estimated that one of every two families in our country experiences some form of domestic violence each year. And one family in five experiences this on a consistent basis.[4]

Abuse is any behavior that is designed to control and/or subjugate another person through the use of fear, humiliation and verbal or physical assaults. "Physical" refers to brutal physical contact rather than accidental contact. It can include pushing, grabbing, shoving, slapping, kicking, biting, choking, punching, hitting with an object, sexual assault or attacking with a knife or a gun.

But there is emotional abuse, as well. Scare tactics, insults, yelling (shouting), temper tantrums, name-calling and continuous criticism fall into this classification. Withholding privileges or affection and/or constantly blaming also fall into this category.

Surprised? You may be. Some feel this is just the way people live. But such a lifestyle is neither appropriate nor healthy. It may be common today, but you need to be forewarned. As you read these definitions you may discover that you grew up in a home that was abusive. Or you may be in an abusive relationship now. Are there any signs of a pattern of abuse in your own life or that of the other person in your relationship?

There are some indications to be aware of for the potential of abuse. Those who come from a home in which they experienced a violent and abusive childhood are more likely to be abusive in their own relationships. Another characteristic of those who abuse is difficulty in expressing feelings with words.

And men do struggle with this more than women. Numerous studies indicate that abusive men are usually nonassertive away from home and struggle with low self-esteem. Because they feel bad about themselves by not living up to our society's portrayal of what a man should be away from home, they often exceed what is normal behavior and become abusive inside the home.

Also, those who abuse often have a desire to dominate. They often believe they are to be the absolute, autocratic ruler in a relationship.

Does what has been discussed so far describe anyone you know? (For additional information on anger and abuse see *When Anger Hits Home* by H. Norman Wright and Dr. Gary Oliver.)

It's important to recall what God's Word has to say about anger:

> If you are angry, don't sin by nursing your grudge. Don't let the sun go down with you still angry—get over it quickly; stop being mean, bad-tempered and angry. Quarreling,

harsh words, and dislike of others should have no place in your lives (Eph. 4:26,31, *TLB*).

It is better to eat soup with someone you love than steak with someone you hate (Prov. 15:17, *TLB*).

Stop your anger! Turn off your wrath. Don't fret and worry—it only leads to harm (Ps. 37:8, *TLB*).

Jealousy is more dangerous and cruel than anger (Prov. 27:4, *TLB*).

Better to live in the desert than with a quarrelsome, complaining woman (Prov. 21:19, *TLB*).

It is better to be slow-tempered than famous; it is better to have self-control than to control an army (Prov. 16:32, *TLB*).

Don't be quick-tempered—that is being a fool (Eccles. 7:9, *TLB*).

Remember that in a relationship acknowledged anger is proper, for it gives you the opportunity to come to grips with its cause. Most anger arises because we're hurt, afraid or frustrated; it is not helpful to "stuff" an emotion that can indicate the presence of such negatives.

But the expression of anger is appropriate only when it doesn't conflict with fulfilling God's purpose in our lives.[5]

Relationship or Situation?
One last thought. Be sure that you're in a *relationship* rather than a *situation*. Do you know the difference? One has potential; the other is a dead-end street. A relationship has the potential for, and includes, commitment. A situation has, well, not much except getting together with the other person.

Perhaps the following questions will help you determine the

difference. Answer each one in the space provided.

1. Are you embarrassed or proud about your involvement with this person?_____

2. Do you let others know about your involvement or keep it hush-hush because of what others would think or say?_____
Describe:

_____

_____

_____

_____

_____

3. Do you jump to the conclusion that you have to point out this person's attributes whenever anyone else finds out about the two of you? Are you defensive about him/her?

_____

_____

4. Do you sense or already know there's no future with this person, but you stay together for the wrong reasons?_____

5. Do you sense that this isn't right for you? _____
If yes, describe why:

_____

_____

_____

6. Do you sense that you have more to offer to the relationship than the other person? _____
If yes, describe:

_____

_____

_____

7. Is the other person involved with anyone else, breaking off a relationship or on the rebound?[6] _____
If yes, how is this affecting you?

_____

_____

_____

_____

_____

Notes

1. Carolyn N. Bushong, *Seven Dumbest Relationship Mistakes Smart People Make* (New York: Villard Books, 1997), pp. 152-172. Adapted.
2. Miriam Elliot and Susan Mettzner, *The Perfectionist Predicament* (New York: William Morrow and Co., 1991), pp. 262-263. Adapted.
3. H. Norman Wright and Gary J. Oliver, *How to Bring out the Best in Your Spouse* (Chicago: Moody Press, 1994), pp. 206-212 Adapted.
4. Matthew McKay, Peter D. Rogers and Judith McKay, *When Anger Hurts* (Oakland, Calif.: New Harbinger Publications, 1989), p. 270. Adapted.
5. Lawrence J. Crabb, *The Marriage Builder* (Grand Rapids: Zondervan Publishing House, 1982). Adapted.
6. Lauri Langford, *If It's Love You Want, Why Settle for Just Sex?* (Rocklin, Calif.: Prima Publishing, 1996), p. 21. Adapted.

$$\textcircled{8}$$

The Fear That Cripples a Relationship

≈

*Doubts and fears about relationships can be
dealt with by completing the Couples Relationship
Historical Sketch and other inventories
discussed in this chapter.*

Have you ever seen movies of birds engaging in a courtship dance? They're fascinating and funny. The awkward fowls fluff up their feathers, prance around, dance toward one another, and then retreat. They do this time after time until the courtship ritual is finished. Then they get together.

Some people are like this. They move close to a person, but then retreat. Their relationship pattern is a constant pattern of moving closer, then moving away. There seems to be both a strong desire for a lasting relationship, and at the same time an odd reluctance.

"Ambivalence" is another way to describe this situation. If this characterizes you, you're familiar with the phrase, "Can't you ever make up your mind?" The inability to decide is a killer when it comes to relationships. With ambivalence as your guide, what you're doing is operating on the belief that by not making up your mind—by holding out long enough—you'll eventually make the right decision.

In reality, however, this is a protective move to keep you from taking a risk. An ambivalent person is looking for a guarantee—a certainty of being right. It's a battle between the heart and the head. Once again, it is fear that underlies this difficulty.

Fears Both Said and Silent

Many singles experience thoughts and feelings such as the following. Have you felt them yourself?

"I don't think this relationship will be reciprocated. My friend's needs will be met, but mine won't."

"This relationship takes so much work. I'm afraid I can't balance the needs I have for closeness as well as independence."

"I'm afraid of opening up any more. Why? The more he knows about me, the greater the possibility of rejection. I can't handle that."

"If I stay in this relationship I could be controlled."

"If she meets my family, she'll discover what a weird bunch I come from. It will make her wonder about me."

"What if she becomes too dependent on me?"

"I'm not sure a marriage will be worth giving up the freedom I like so much!"[1]

Being married carries with it both freedoms and limitations. I've talked with men and women who have been in and out of one relationship after another for 25 years. They say they want a lasting relationship, and have been close to someone at times, but one or both decide not to make that final dance toward intimacy. It's as though they would rather hold on to their freedom of singleness than exchange it for the freedoms of marriage. They are in some ways driven by fear.

For many it's a commitment conflict rather than not being able to find anyone. It's good to approach a lifelong relationship with caution, but some seem downright phobic.

Sometimes relationships are characterized by an overwhelming ambivalence. On the one hand the person loves the other and can say it. They may say it very freely at the beginning of a relationship—but their safeguard to keeping themselves from marriage is in the word "but." Those whose hesitation forms a pattern, and who live with the fear of commitment, often make such statements as:

"I love you, but we're so different it would never work."
"I love you, but I think I need more time."
"I love you, but I just don't deserve you."
"I love you, but I have too many other issues to work out first."
"I love you, but I need to be alone right now."
"I love you, but I'm interested in others as well."
"I love you, but I'm not sure I'm *in love* with you. Do you understand?"

These lines play over and over inside of hesitant people's minds. Only infrequently are they expressed to their partners. And even if they are, usually the other one hears the "I love you," not the "but."[2]

Guide to Assessing Your Fears

How can you determine whether you or the person you're interested in has a high level of fear when it comes to making a commitment? Consider the following characteristics, which are in the form of personal questions.

1. **Do you or your partner have a history of relationships in which one wants more and the other less?**
This could take the form of more time, closeness or commitment. As you consider the relationships you've been in or currently have, do you want more or less? What about your partner?

Do either of you complain that the other pulls back or withholds?

Do either of you limit how much is given in order to avoid intimacy?

Do either of you have a pattern of hurting or disappointing partners?

Is one a bit anxious because the other is not giving the security he or she needs?

≈ Couples who are out-of-synch may never get together. When one moves closer, the other moves away. It's a dance in which the two are always out of step. ≈

Is one pushing the other for more commitment?

On the following scale, indicate where you are in terms of commitment, and also where you think your partner is:

	0	25%	50%	75%	100%
	(Forget it!)				(Yes! I'm all for it!)
Me	⊢----------+----------+----------+----------⊣				
My Partner	⊢----------+----------+----------+----------⊣				

Sometimes it's difficult for couples who are out of synch to ever get together. When one moves closer the other may move away. It becomes a dance in which the two are always out of step.

2. **Have you ever experienced a significant relationship that came to a halt because you or your partner became too fearful of moving ahead?**

If this occurred, do you know if it was a feeling of panic or a steady sense of fear? Who was the person that was rejected? Was this the first time, or a pattern?

3. **Have you experienced a relationship in which either**

you or your partner set limitations of some kind on closeness and intimacy (nonsexual)?

Some people are so structured, so cautious, so compartmentalized, that you'd think they invented boundaries! Their concerns may appear so legitimate that you're unaware that it's actually a fear of involvement. It may appear to be caution or simple logistics.

A person may limit his time and availability. He may exclude you from specific areas of his life such as family functions, work, social occasions, certain friends, or even his church. I've seen some individuals who attended the same church, but the man made it a point never to be seen there together. He didn't want them to be known as a couple. There's a real message in that! A person like this may not want to share other special occasions or even special interests. He or she may even set restrictions on how much money you spend together on outings, or limit gifts to cards. All of these steps seem to have the purpose of maintaining a certain distance in relationships.

If you or your partner tend to do this, don't guess about the motivation. It's clear. Excluding and being excluded won't help a relationship to grow.

4. **Do you have a tendency to develop relationships when, down deep, you know they would never work out—that the person just doesn't have what is needed for a relationship?**

Some people do this so they will always end up with an escape clause. Usually the difficulties are there to begin with, but they are overlooked or rationalized. They could be differences involving political views, social status, race, age, levels of Christian commitment, or even Christian vs. non-Christian. It's an attitude that says, "There is too much of this for it to ever work."

Differences will be in every relationship; but a pattern of seeking them carries a sign saying, "Watch out!"

5. **Do you believe there is that "one and only right person" for you out there somewhere, but as you look, the person you actually find is never quite right?**

Once again this can be a signal that you seek someone with "too much" of a negative in his or her life. You just haven't found the "right person" (and probably never will).

6. **Do you or your partner have a tendency to seek out those who are unavailable for one reason or another?**
It could be they're unavailable relationally. They're involved with someone else, but you're still attracted—*as well as safe*. There can be no commitment with someone whose heart is really elsewhere.

Some potential partners are geographically unavailable. You meet someone at a resort or on a plane, and when you're together it's great. You write, e-mail, fax and phone each other; but the distance adds to the romance rather than the reality.

> ≈ Every relationship is a learning experience—if you let it become one. ≈

There are pros and cons to some long-distance relationships. Some couples have said they put more energy and thought into building the relationship than they would if they were together all the time. And they say they don't take each other for granted.

But if you marry without several months of spending time together in the same locale, it can be an intense adjustment. Some say that when the relationship stops being long-distance it can even precipitate a crisis.

In some ways it is reminiscent of the adjustments required by those in the armed services when they are deployed for six months to another area. Many marriages experience major adjustments and crises when the serviceman returns to his family. It takes weeks to settle back into a normal routine. So if you're involved in a long-distance relationship, be aware of the crisis potential when you eventually find yourselves in the same area.

Working side by side with this person for three months—seeing them under all kinds of stresses and conditions—will clue you in to reality!

I've seen some people who seem purposely to connect with what I call the "permanently unavailable." It gives them a good basis for commitment to be illusive.

Perhaps you can identify other reasons for someone to avoid commitment. And perhaps this doesn't apply to you or the other person. But it's something to consider.[3]

Relationship Historical Sketches

Every relationship is a learning experience. That is, if you let it become one. You can learn not only from each relationship but from the pattern of your relationships. Have you ever completed a Relationship Historical Sketch on yourself? It can be very revealing.

For example, Jim was 35 when he said he wanted to talk about getting married. Actually, he wanted to find out why he wasn't already married by now. He dated most of the time, but nothing seemed to work out. I suggested that we spend some time creating a history of his dating or relationship patterns, starting with the first person he was involved with and continuing all the way up to the present. This is what Jim's relational history looked like:

1st date	1st relationship	2nd relationship
Age 17	Ages 18-19	Ages 22-23
Prom (had to go)	She broke up with me.	Both called it off.

3rd relationship	4th relationship	5th relationship
Ages 24-25	Ages 27-29	Ages 30-32
She pursued me, but I lost interest.	I cared for this woman, but she left me for another man.	I could see it wouldn't work, so why waste time?

6th relationship	7th relationship	8th relationship
Age 32	Age 33	Age 34
I liked her but she traveled too much.	Not sure why I stopped calling her. She was still interested.	Wouldn't have worked out. Values were too different.

9th relationship	10th relationship	Currently
Age 34	Age 35	Age 35
She was talking marriage after a month.	Not sure why we stopped seeing each other.	No one at this time.

After Jim completed this history I asked him to reflect on the chart for the next week and try to determine what the pattern of his relationships is telling him. This is what he said:

"After looking at this I decided I sure didn't want any woman to see this or she'd be frightened off immediately. Putting this in writing had a totally different impact on me than just thinking about it. It's so flaky. Or I felt kind of flaky about my relationship life! I realized I was kind of cautious, but maybe I'm picky. The more I read this the more I realized I've been burned or hurt by some of my experiences.

"I guess I'm gun-shy and protective. I'm okay about the first four relationships. I invested enough time in them to make an evaluation. But my pattern over the last four years! Regardless of the reasons, I bailed out! You know what I said to myself? Basically, for each one I said, 'Why invest more time? It will never work.' But that's not true. Perhaps I was afraid it would work. I'm the one who's afraid of what it would mean to commit. Maybe I don't have what it takes. I guess I'm at the place where I've got to come to grips with my pattern if I'm ever going to be capable of marriage."

Jim took the time to look at his life and to make some important discoveries. This may be a step you'd like to take. It could be you're already in a serious relationship and wondering if this is the one for you.

It may be time for both of you to complete a *Couples Relationship Historical Sketch* (CRHS). The CRHS has been adapted from a process used for engaged couples by Dr. Robert F. Stahmann and Dr. William J. Hiebert. It's designed to discover significant relational events, dates, interactions, conflicts, and growth. It will help you clearly discover how you behave with each other, what each contributes to the relationship, how you affect one another and any patterns you've already established.

The following is an example of a CRHS of a couple we'll call Sandy and Jim.

Sandy, age 26	Met each other 4/94	First date 7/94
Jim, age 24	Served on two committees for three months.	Dinner and walk on beach. Talked for seven hours.

Second date 7/94	Three major conflicts (two resolved)	11/94
	Saw each other four to six times a week.	

11/94 – 6/95	7/95	7/97
Separated. Mutually agreed upon.	Relationship resumed. Exclusive.	Sandy gave ultimatum: marriage or let's go our separate ways.

Of course the pattern of everyone's CRHS will be different. Your relational history will be more meaningful if you will take the time to reflect on it by means of the following Relationship Assessment Inventory. The process of answering the questions will help to clarify the development of your relationship, especially if you take the time to discuss your individual responses. The inventory will help you determine where you are in the relationship and what needs to happen before you move ahead.

Take a large sheet of paper and answer and discuss the following questions:

1. Where and how did you meet?
2. What was your initial impression of each other?
3. If you were friends before you began dating, how did you make the transition to romance?

4. Describe your first date—where, what, when, who asked who, etc.

5. What was your impression of your partner after your first date?

6. How did you decide you wanted to continue seeing your partner after the first date? Who decided where you went and what you did? Who was the decision-maker at this time? Is it the same now?

7. When did you decide to date one another exclusively? How was the decision made? Was it discussed or did it just happen?

8. What were your initial concerns about the other person? What are they now?

9. When was the first conflict? What was it about? How was it resolved? Was this satisfactory to you?

10. When did you first discover something you wanted to change about the other person? How did you approach it? Did you succeed?

11. Have you experienced a separation? If so, describe the reason for it and who initiated it. What did it accomplish, and what brought you back together?[4]

Up to now, we've dealt with the past—your relational history. The following questions are designed to help you assess the current status of your relationship. On another large sheet of paper answer and discuss the following:

1. Describe how much significant time you spend together and when you spend it.

2. Describe five behaviors or tasks your partner does that you appreciate.

3. List five personal qualities of your partner that you appreciate.

4. How frequently do you affirm or reinforce each other for the behaviors and qualities described in questions 2 and 3?

5. List four important requests you have for your partner at this time.
6. How frequently do you make these requests?
7. What is your partner's response?
6. List four important requests your partner has for you at this time.
7. How frequently does he/she make these requests?
8. What is your response?
9. What do you appreciate most about your partner's style of communication?
10. What frustrates you most about your partner's communication?

Since this last issue, communication, is so basic to your relationship, expand your assessment of it by completing the following special communications inventory.

Communication in Your Relationship

Answer each question with one of these responses: *Myself, My Partner* or *Neither.*

1. Listens when the other person is talking   _____
2. Appears to understand the other when they share _____
3. Tends to amplify and say too much   _____
4. Tends to condense and say too little   _____
5. Tends to keep feelings to oneself   _____
6. Tends to be critical or to nag   _____
7. Encourages the other   _____
8. Tends to withdraw when confronted   _____
9. Holds in hurts and becomes resentful   _____
10. Lets the other have their say without interrupting _____
11. Remains silent for long periods of time when the other is angry   _____
12. Fears expressing disagreement if the other becomes angry   _____

13. Expresses appreciation for what is done most of the time   _____

14. Complains that the other person doesn't understand him/her   _____

15. Can disagree without losing temper   _____

16. Tends to monopolize the conversation   _____

17. Feels free to discuss sexual standards and beliefs with one's partner   _____

18. Gives compliments and makes nice comments to the other   _____

19. Feels misunderstood by one's partner   _____

20. Tends to avoid discussions of feelings   _____

21. Avoids discussing specific problem topics or issues _____

Which of the above would you like to change, and what will you do to accomplish that?

Following are two other inventories that will help you come to terms with your relationship.

Current Level of Satisfaction

To indicate your current level of satisfaction, place an X at the appropriate place on the scale, with 0 indicating no satisfaction. A score of 5 is average, and 10 means super, fantastic—the best! Then go over the statements again using a circle to indicate what you think your partner's level of satisfaction is at the present time.

1. Our personal involvement with each other, when we see one another

   0   1   2   3   4   5   6   7   8   9   10

2. Our affectionate and romantic interaction

   0   1   2   3   4   5   6   7   8   9   10

3. My trust in my partner

   0   1   2   3   4   5   6   7   8   9   10

4. My partner's trust in me

   0   1   2   3   4   5   6   7   8   9   10

5. The depth of our communication together

   0   1   2   3   4   5   6   7   8   9   10

6. How well we speak one another's language

   0   1   2   3   4   5   6   7   8   9   10

7. The way we make decisions

   0   1   2   3   4   5   6   7   8   9   10

8. The way we manage conflict

   0   1   2   3   4   5   6   7   8   9   10

9. Adjustment to one another's differences

   0   1   2   3   4   5   6   7   8   9   10

10. Our church involvement

   0   1   2   3   4   5   6   7   8   9   10

11. The way we support each other in rough times

   0   1   2   3   4   5   6   7   8   9   10

12. Our spiritual interaction

   0   1   2   3   4   5   6   7   8   9   10

The Future of This Relationship

Be sure to discuss each partner's responses to these important questions.

1. If this relationship were to fail, I would feel _____

_____

_____

2. If this relationship were to fail, my partner would feel

_____

_____

3. My commitment level to staying in this relationship is:

Little or no commitment					Average commitment					Absolute commitment
0	1	2	3	4	5	6	7	8	9	10

4. My partner's commitment level to staying in this relationship is:

Little or no commitment					Average commitment					Absolute commitment
0	1	2	3	4	5	6	7	8	9	10

Hopefully, having answered these questions, you will have a better understanding of your relationship. If your relationship is moving toward marriage, you may want to begin pre-engagement or premarital counseling. Some couples spend eight to 10 hours with a qualified pastor or counselor and complete 60 to 80 hours of homework. That may sound like a big-time investment, and it is. But why not? Especially if you're planning to be married for the rest of your life![5]

Notes
1. Michæl S. Broder, *The Art of Staying Together* (New York: Hyperion, 1993), pp. 25, 26. Adapted.
2. Steven Carter and Julia Sokol, *He's Scared, She's Scared* (New York: Dell Publishers, 1993), pp. 127, 128. Adapted.
3. Ibid., pp. 18-25. Adapted.
4. Robert F. Stahmann and William J. Hiebert, *Premarital Counseling* (Lexington, Mass.: Lexington Books/D.C. Heath & Co., 1987), pp. 64-70. Adapted.
5. H. Norman Wright, "Marital Assessment Inventory." Adapted.

$$\textcircled{9}$$

How to Fall Out of Love
(It Happens, but It Doesn't Have To!)

≈

Love can die for both dating and married couples.
Here's how to recognize—and treat—symptoms
that can lead to the death of your relationship.

Would you like to learn how to fall out of love? Probably not. But wait before you judge that question too harshly. Many people *do* fall out of love before *and* after they marry. Most of them didn't want to, but it happened. And it could have been avoided if they had known the process they must go through in order to see their love die. This is a painful process even in a dating relationship. It's even more painful when it happens after you're married.

It really isn't difficult to predict which relationships are most likely to have one person fall out of love with his or her partner. When you fall out of love with someone it usually means you have a high degree of relationship dissatisfaction. Hopefully this chapter can help you recognize the beginning phases of this process, and thus avoid the experience.

When the death of love begins, there is a gradual loss of emotional attachment toward the other person. It's not enjoyable, either for the one whose love is dying or for his or her partner. Your caring for the other person drops off. That in itself can be a scary feeling for you. You begin to ask, "What's wrong with me?"

A gulf begins to grow between the two of you. It's called emotional distancing. And worse yet, you come to the place where all you feel toward the other is apathy and indifference. You've shut down and shut off. You may not feel good about what's happening to you, but it's important to recognize these signs.

Remember, the death of love is both *predictable* and *preventable.*

Disillusionment

The initial phase of falling out of love is *disillusionment.* In any relationship there will be a degree of this feeling. It's not all bad, either. Coming down to reality and breaking out of any infatuation is a necessity. It's actually better to go through this prior to marriage so you can sort things out. It can be a severe shock when it happens after marriage.

Why do we become disillusioned? Expectations. The higher the level of expectations, the more you're building your relationship on idealism. And the more your expectations aren't met, the greater the depth of your disappointment. I've seen this happen both in dating and marriage relationships. It's the feeling that says, "What I thought I was getting isn't what I got!" It's a big letdown. Watch out for your expectations. They have the potential to be killers.

To eliminate this problem you need to identify the expectations you have for the other person before you marry as well as after. In premarital counseling I have each person write out 25 expectations they have for their partner after they marry, and then exchange their lists.

I wish I had a video camera to record the surprised look on their faces as they discover what their partners expect. The discussion that follows is usually lively and informative. Sometimes it's through this process that you discover *it's just not going to work.*

Here is a listing of one man's expectations. As you can imagine, his fiancée checked several that she felt unsure about being able to fulfill.

1. Personal daily Bible study—at least five days a week.
2. I take care of finances (paying bills on time—not late); we get weekly allowances.
3. Faithful sexuality.
4. Exercise three times a week (one-half hour each).
5. Own a dog and allow him to roam in living room (but not on the furniture).
6. Allow me to keep guns and not sell them.
7. Equal participating in household chores (hire a house cleaner once a week).
8. Have two or three children.
9. She does not work while any of the children are under age 5 and not in school.
10. Never nag.
11. Allow me to work out and go to exercise classes at least one day a week.
12. Encourage me to study.
13. Take the time to consider and listen to words and activities.
14. Have summit meetings every three months.
15. Eat one meal together daily if possible.
16. We buy one major thing at a time.
17. Credit cards are for *emergencies* only!
18. Nothing disturbs our meals together (phone off the hook).
19. My clothes mended within two weeks.
20. Dishes done daily.

Fears and Concerns

Another area that is somewhat related to expectations and disillusionment has to do with the fears and concerns you may have about marriage. Since we hear so much about the potential problems in marriage, we may enter it with certain fears. And fears often tie in to expectations.

≈ Discuss your expectations with your partner before you marry. If you consider certain items to be "must haves" in a relationship, it's only fair to let the other person know. ≈

Here is a list of fears one 22-year-old woman brought to the third session of premarital counseling. Note how they relate to expectations.

My Fears and Anxieties Entering Marriage

1. That we will be too busy to have quality time for each other.
2. I will not be able to keep him and my mother happy—she will have her feelings hurt.
3. His priority for working out and exercising will still be greater than mine.
4. We will not have devotions or prayer together *every* day.
5. There will be times when I will want to go into debt for a particular item and he will not.
6. After a few years of marriage I will not want to give in and will want to "have it out."
7. I will want to concentrate on my career when he would rather be having a family.
8. I may want to decorate the house a little more formal than casual.
9. I'll want to buy a new car—he'll want to buy a used one.
10. I will get pregnant before we plan to.

How do you think these would affect their marriage?

Expectations are also affected when people change. Your partner may change from the way he was prior to marriage; or your perception of him can change. If you expect your partner to be who he is after you marry, discuss it beforehand. If certain items are critical "must haves" in a relationship, it's only fair to let the other person know.

When changes strike your marriage they can play tricks with your mind. You begin to think of your partner in terms that are more negative than positive. You may begin to have doubts about him and about the permanency potential for your relationship.

The negative thoughts you nurse can lead to many forms of blame. It could be self-blame—you think the problem is you. And women do tend to blame themselves more than men do. Or most of the blame may be directed toward the other person. This in turn reinforces your feelings of disillusionment.

This is a common problem that does not have to occur! Taking plenty of time to get to know the other person, talking in-depth and discovering and evaluating the expectations both of you have can be deterrents.

Hurt

When your feelings begin to die for the other person, the next phase you experience is *hurt*. You'll experience occasional episodes of hurt in any dating relationships. But when love is on the downward path, hurt feels like a constant, low-grade fever.

The feelings in this phase include loneliness, being treated unfairly and unjustly by the other person, and a sense of loss— although you may not identify it or perceive it as a loss.

This is when your mind swings into high gear with its pro- grammed tendency to focus on the negatives.

My partner just doesn't understand me. That's unfair. He/she should understand.

My needs are not being met and they should be.

My partner must not think I'm very important or he/she would be acting differently.

Persons suffering in this phase frequently begin to think about what the relationship is costing them. They also wonder what they are getting out of it. Usually they feel they have ended up with the short end of the stick. Have you been there yet?

The Negative Nature

This is where our "old nature" begins to show itself. We all have an inclination toward negative thinking. We all talk to ourselves. That's a given. But too often, unfortunately, the content of this "self-talk" is negative.

Mankind has struggled with this since Genesis 6:5. "The Lord saw that the wickedness of man was great in the earth, and that every imagination and intention of all human thinking was only evil continually" (*Amp.*).

Scripture again and again points out the importance of our thoughts and how they need to be controlled.

"As he thinketh in his heart, so is he" (Prov. 23:7, *KJV*).

"The thoughts of the righteous are right: but the counsels of the wicked are deceit" (Prov. 12:5, *KJV*).

"Search me, O God, and know my heart; test me and know my thoughts" (Ps. 139:23, *RSV*).

"Gird your minds for action" (1 Pet. 1:13, *NASB*).

In Bible times, soldiers would "gird their loins" for battle. To "gird your minds" means deliberately putting out of the mind anything that could hinder the Christian life. There's a strong interrelationship among your thoughts, feelings and behaviors, which reinforces the feelings and thoughts. And then the cycle repeats: The feeling intensifies or reinforces a particular thinking pattern and thus the behavior.

Thoughts, positive or negative, grow stronger when fertilized with constant repetition. That may explain why so many who are gloomy and gray stay in that mood, and why others who are cheery and enthusiastic continue to be so, even in the midst of difficult circumstances. Please do not misunderstand. Happiness (like winning) is a matter of right thinking, not intelligence, age or position. Our performance is directly related to the thoughts we deposit in our memory bank. We can only draw on what we deposit.

What kind of performance would your car deliver if every morning before you left for work you scooped up a handful of dirt and put it in your crankcase? The fine-tuned engine would soon be coughing and sputtering. Ultimately, it would refuse to start. The same is true of your life. Thoughts about yourself and attitudes toward others that are narrow, destructive and abrasive produce wear and tear on your mental motor. They send you off the road while others drive past.[1]

To salve hurt feelings, you may begin to gripe and complain to others about how dissatisfying your relationship is. Attempts to change the relationship and make it better, as well as attempts to change your partner, emerge. Personally I believe we can and need to help one another change. But when you approach it from a position of hurt, you usually use an approach that either reinforces the basic problem or makes it worse.

Anger

How do you respond when you're hurt? The most common response, *anger*, is the third phase of this process of killing love in a relationship.

Anger can overlap the hurt phase and be closely intertwined. Anger also arises when expectations are unfulfilled. The frustration that occurs is one step away from anger. These two go hand in hand.

Again, anger isn't all bad. It's often a helpful protective response. It helps us overcome our feelings of vulnerability and helplessness when we've been hurt. Anger has its place in our lives, and it can be effective; but all too often it's not.

Anger wears many faces. It can be a slow, steady burn or it can be expressed as strongly as a heat-seeking missile. Anger is a sense of irritation. It's a feeling of strong displeasure. Listen to this description of what anger does.

Anger stuns. It frightens. It makes people feel bad about themselves. And of course it warns them to stop doing whatever is offending you. But people gradually become injured and resistant and as soon as they see you, they put on their emotional armor in preparation for the next upset. The more anger you express, the less effective your anger becomes, the less you are listened to and the more cut off you may begin to feel from genuine closeness.[2]

Have you experienced what was just described? Unfortunately, many of us have. Often our purpose in becoming angry is to draw the other person closer to us. But it has just the opposite effect—it pushes them away. After all, who wants to get close to an angry person?

This is the time when the phrase, "I think I'm falling out of love," begins to emerge. As the disappointment and hurt continue, you tend to obscure the love that was there when you began.

The feelings of this stage can best be described as resentment, indignation or bitterness. And these deaden feelings of love. If anger is continually smoldering it tends to diminish the quality of love, and in time resentment gains a foothold. Resentment is an eroding disease that feeds on lingering anger for its lifeblood. Resentment eats away at the relationship until the love is dead. Worse, if resentment continues it eventually can produce hate—and hate separates, driving the other person away.

One man told me that his resentment took several years to develop. "I could never please my wife," he said. "I completed task after task that she asked me to do, and not once did I receive a compliment or a word of thanks. My resentment came from my anger, which was really intense." His final words revealed that his marriage had become a shell: "Now my resentment has subsided, and I have no feelings for her at all."

A wife told me about her anger over her husband's demands. "Every now and then I want to get back at him and make him pay for what he's said," she confided. "That frightens me since I know it's the beginning of anger."

Both of these people have been offended. Their anger is deep, and the results range from feelings of revenge to no feelings at all.

When you are caught up in this cycle you will have an abundance of thoughts to reinforce it. Trust is just about gone. You now look at the accumulation of hurts, and you feel their combined impact. Your focus is on what your partner has done or hasn't done, and blame is a consistent thought. Again, as you think about the other person, negative thoughts outweigh the positive.

He doesn't love me.

Why did I ever think she would love me? She doesn't even say it or show it. Sometimes I could just throttle her.

Sometimes I wish he'd have an accident. He deserves it.

With feelings and thoughts like this, you can imagine how a person might behave at this time. By now the feelings are being expressed to your partner—not in a way that draws the two of you closer, but in a way that tends to alienate the two of you.

Expressions of hurt, anger and disappointment are usually presented in a critical way. They're mingled with an attitude of disgust. It's not uncommon to avoid the other person. There is physical and emotional withdrawal from both the partner and the relationship. If you're married, it's even worse. A wife said, "How is it possible to physically respond to someone you've started to loathe? I can't even sleep in the same bed with him because I'm so angry at him."

This is a dangerous time in a person's life. Hurt and anger make us vulnerable to finding need-fulfillment elsewhere. In the death of love, emotional desperation grows, and this is a major starting point for affairs in marriage. The lack of need-fulfillment and intimacy creates an intense vacuum. It contributes to alienation as well as resentment.

Here is a graphic description of what a person experiences at this time:

It's a cold feeling in the pit of your stomach. One day, perhaps after a fight or after one more disappointment, you look at your spouse and think, *I've made a terrible, terrible mistake. I married the wrong person.*

For anyone who places a high value on the vows of marriage, or who has children who would be deeply hurt by a divorce, that's a terrifying conclusion.

Still, it's a feeling that most people—even people with deep convictions about the sanctity of marriage—have had at one time or another. For some, it's a fleeting sensation brought on by passing fantasies of what it would have been like if they had married that high school sweetheart. But for others, the doubts are serious. Scary. Persistent.

When these doubts come, and don't go away, it's usually because the feelings you once had have diminished—or died altogether. Feelings of closeness, tenderness and sexual attraction are a distant memory, replaced by feelings of resentment, alienation, anger, perhaps even disgust.

For most people, the doubts begin with tiny hints, fleeting thoughts. *I wonder what my life would have been like if I had married my old boyfriend? I bet he wouldn't take me for granted like my husband does!* Sometimes the good feelings are simply neutralized, replaced only by a numbness. Sometimes they are malignantly transformed, like healthy cells transmogrified into cancer cells, from feelings of love into feelings of contempt, distrust and despair.

As doubt grows, so does the evidence that you made the wrong choice of a mate: Your spouse has unchangeable character flaws. Someone else makes you feel better than he/she does. You can't stop fighting. Your values are incompatible. You have different views about child-rearing. You're ill-suited sexually. There's no more passion. Your family backgrounds are too disparate. You're at different places spiritually. Your careers are pulling you apart. There's no more respect or trust between you. You can't communicate. You're always angry. You're bored. You're numb. You're constantly on the defensive.

Doubt can quickly turn into panic. *Time is passing— will my entire life be wasted because I made the wrong choice?* Panic is often accompanied by depression. The future looks hopeless. Nothing fits. Nothing makes sense. Nothing can be counted on anymore.[3]

Ambivalence

The fourth phase of love's loss is *ambivalence.* Feelings at this time reflect a sense of turmoil, as they shift back and forth between despair and hope for both the relationship and the person. We're indecisive and unsure about what to do.

This state is reflected in our thoughts as well. We wonder, *What will it take for this relationship to work? Would it be best to just get out of this? I don't see it going anywhere.* We consider other options to staying with this person, but we are also aware of and think about how the breakup would affect us and others, especially if it's a divorce.

These feelings and thoughts lead to all sorts of behaviors. Sometimes friends and relatives are made aware of what is occurring, and there may be consideration of another who might be a better choice than the current partner. Once again, remember that these phases can overlap and it can all add up to a state of confusion.

The Death of Love

The final phase is what all this has been leading up to: disaffection, or the *death of love.* The only feelings left are those that reflect the death of what each hoped would be a happy, fulfilling relationship. Love has been replaced by indifference, detachment and apathy, if not downright loathing. Some of the thoughts at this time are:

I've had it. Enough is enough. Why knock myself out anymore over this relationship? Nothing I did worked and now it's history.

I have nothing left to feel with. I'm numb. I never thought it would come to this. But six years is long enough to invest and not see any returns.

I can't even get angry at her anymore. There's nothing left to feel with!

Thoughts like these simply reflect the feelings. There's no desire to be with the other person. The relationship is a closed book. Avoidance is what you want now—at all costs.

The love that once existed...is dead.[4]

Hope for Healing

Fortunately, not all couples experience the pattern of dying love described in this chapter. Why do some love relationships die

≈ There are ways to prevent love from dying, and even ways to reverse the process. God does have a future for relationships. ≈

and others live on? Are there any patterns or predictors that can be used to help avoid those behaviors that are so destructive?

I hear this question frequently from young couples. It's a good question, and there is good news. There are ways to prevent love from dying, and even ways to reverse the process. God does have a future for relationships, but it must be a cooperative effort on the part of God, the man and the woman.

Marriage Killers
In the movies we've all seen stories about hitmen, assassins, terminators, etc. They're all killers. We see them in relationships and marriages as well. They include getting married at the physical and romantic stage, never developing friendship love, not understanding and blending your differences. Research indicates the presence of other killers as well.

Lack of mutuality. One of the main contributing factors to the death of love is a lack of mutual appreciation of each other. This can involve a variety of behaviors, including overt acts of controlling one's spouse through disregard of his or her unique personality qualities, opinions, faith, desires, activities or lifestyle.

The lack of mutuality may involve forcing one's partner to do something against his or her will. It may include criticism, blame and put-downs.

The desire to control. The behaviors and attitudes mentioned above are all control tactics. Control comes in many forms and disguises. As we have seen, perfectionists have a tendency to want to control others.

A wife married for 10 years described her life:

> Carl is just so critical and particular, but not in a loud or angry way. He never raises his voice. But he looks at me, shakes his head, or rolls his eyes to show his disgust over what I've done. If not that, I get what I call the "soft lecture." He doesn't raise his voice, get angry or sound firm. Rather, he talks in a soft, patient condescending tone of voice implying, "How could you have been so stupid?" Sometimes I get the silent treatment and some sighs. That's the signal for me to figure out what I've done wrong.
>
> There have even been times, believe it or not, when he has taken the fork out of my mouth because I'm eating too much, turned off the TV because I shouldn't be watching that program, or corrected my volume of talking in public. I'm tired of it. I'm tired of going along with what he's doing. I can't deny who I am and I can't live trying to figure out how to please him. Besides, I've heard this so much I've begun to doubt myself. I've even thought, *Maybe he's right. Maybe I need to do what he says. Maybe I am creating the problems.* But fortunately I came to my senses.[5]

What about you? Have you experienced a relationship in which the other person controlled you? Or do you tend to be a controller? Control destroys love. It's not a biblical pattern.

Lack of empathy. When one is a controller, one of the key ingredients of mutuality in a relationship will be missing—empathy. Regard for others and the ability to enter into their feeling worlds are parts of empathy. With empathy you show you are interested in your partner's world as well as your own. Empathy means entering that world, becoming comfortable with it and refraining from being judgmental about it.

Empathy conveys an exceptionally important message to another person. It says, "You count. You're important and significant." It both validates and encourages the development of the partner's self-esteem. But controllers don't usually care about their partner's feelings.

The absence of intimacy. Intimacy is one of the necessary foundations for the survival of a marriage. Love dies in the absence of intimacy. In marriages like the one described above in which one partner is dominant and the other is passive or submissive, intimacy is impossible. (The word "submissive" in this context is not the healthy, biblical definition, but refers to submission based on fear, inadequacy and insecurity. It's the "keeping peace at any cost" response.)

Obviously, the style of a relationship affects the level of intimacy.

Power and Intimacy
(Power=the capacity to influence another)

Style of Marriage		Level of Intimacy
More or less equal		Deep levels can develop
Dominant-submissive		Intimacy is avoided
Warfare		Intimacy is impossible
Fused		Intimacy is shaky and conditional

The *more or less equal* style of the marriage relationship indicates a balanced power distribution. It is a complementary relationship. Both partners think of themselves as competent, and each sees the other person as competent, too. Each person has specific areas of expertise in which his or her views have greater weight than the other, but this is not threatening to the other person.

If you're in a relationship now, is it more or less equal?

Dominant persons are not about to open their lives and become vulnerable, because it would lessen their sense of power or control. And submissive partners learn not to reveal much, because it will probably be used against them in some way. Not only does the controlling partner restrict you from expressing who you are, you don't want to express yourself because of the repercussions.

In your relationship, who tends to be more dominant and who is more submissive?

Some relationships are explosive, or in a state of active *warfare*. Both husband and wife have the freedom to initiate action, give advice, criticize, etc., but most of their behaviors are competitive. If one states that he has achieved a goal or progressed in some way, the spouse lets it be known that she, too, has attained similar success. Both make it a point to let the other know of his or her equal status.

When conflicts in such a relationship become fairly open and consistent, the relationship is in a warfare state. There is no balance in the relationship because both people are vying for the dominant position and exchanging the same type of behavior.

Finally, there is the *fused* relationship, in which each person shares some power. But in order to have power, each has to give up some individual identity. Separateness does not exist because it seems dangerous; consequently there is an unhealthy type of closeness. Sometimes individuals like this will say, "We are so close that we think alike, we feel alike, and we are completely one."[6]

As we work with couples in premarital counseling, through various tests and evaluation tools, we can now predict in advance the probability that emotional intimacy may be lacking in a relationship and take corrective steps. Sometimes this happens because people have shut down emotionally due to the pain of childhood abuse. In other cases, especially with men, the development of the emotional side of their lives is basically stunted. They haven't been encouraged to develop it.

The lack of intimacy can mean the absence of significant communication, no romance or other signs of distance. When couples marry, one of their desires and one of the characteristics of such a relationship is the opportunity to fling open all the doors and share their innermost feelings. If this opportunity isn't there, love can die.

Hopefully, knowing the patterns described here will help you avoid ever having to experience the death of love in marriage. If love is to die, it's best to have that happen before you marry. Some relationships need to break up. It will be painful, but nothing like the pain of divorce.

Notes

1. Charles Swindoll, *Come Before Winter* (Sisters, Oreg.: Multnomah Books, 1985), p. 239.
2. Matthew McKay, Peter D. Rogers, and Judith McKay, *When Anger Hurts* (Oakland, Calif.: New Harbinger Publications, 1989), p. 33.
3. *What If I Married the Wrong Person?* (Minneapolis: Bethany House Publishers, 1996), pp. 15-16.
4. Karen Kayser, *When Love Dies* (New York: The Guilford Press, 1993), pp. 21-87. Adapted.
5. H. Norman Wright and Gary Oliver, *How to Change Your Spouse (Without Ruining Your Marriage)* (Ann Arbor, Mich.: Servant Publications, 1994), p. 209.
6. Robert Paul Lieberman, Eugene Wheeler and Nancy Sanders, "Behavioral Therapy for Marital Disharmony: an Educational Approach," *Journal of Marriage and Family Counseling* (October 1976), pp. 383-389. Adapted.

Compatibility: Dream or Reality?

≈

Becoming compatible in a relationship is tough if
you're a "colonizer." But if you'll adopt the attitude
of an "immigrant," you'll enjoy the journey.

Do you know what "being compatible" means? It means being capable of living together harmoniously, or getting along well together. It means to be in agreement, to combine well. Compatibility means being mixed together so a relationship enhances, instead of interfering with, the other's capabilities.

If you've ever made a cake (not from a package mix) you'll remember the directions read, "Mix well together." The dry ingredients such as flour, baking soda or powder and salt are sifted together to make sure they are mixed. There are few things more disappointing than biting into a big piece of scrumptious-looking cake only to get a lump of salt or soda that wasn't stirred thoroughly into the mixture. A cake like that, where the ingredients haven't been mixed properly, is something I wouldn't give to my dog.

Compatibility is a major issue in relationships, if not *the* major issue. And what I'm going to say is going to sound like a major contradiction.

First, you and your partner need to be compatible in all areas. Partial compatibility doesn't work very well. Many couples make decisions to share a lifelong relationship only to discover later that there are gaping holes in the relationship. Portions of it are like a wasteland, an arid desert as it were. Nothing grows. Nothing *can* grow.

Second, no couple who marries *is* compatible to begin with. They think they are, and they may have the core ingredients. That's good. But compatibility is a developmental process. It grows. If the basic ingredients are there, it's fairly easy. If not, you're in for an abundance of work and change.

Many couples who question their compatibility will try cohabitation, or "living together," before committing to the legally-binding act of marriage. This is one of the worst mistakes you can make. The popular view is that living together is a legitimate testing ground for marriage. But time and again this great experiment has failed miserably. (For an eye-opening look at the documented results of living together, see appendix II.)

The marriage relationship is really required for two people to become fully compatible. And it usually takes the first 10 years of marriage for compatibility to be refined. (This subject was discussed in *Finding Your Perfect Mate*. The topics of learning styles and knowing God's will were covered there. In this discussion we're going to consider other elements in depth.)

Third, those couples who become compatible have certain characteristics or skills that help them develop compatibility: they flex, stretch, adapt and change. There's no other way. There is no substitute.

The Big Stretch

Perhaps you've seen pictures of the torture devices of the Middle Ages. One favorite of interrogators and tormentors was called "the rack." A person was placed on the rack with his feet tied to one end and his arms outstretched and tied to the other end. A wheel was turned to increase tension, pulling the arms and legs of the poor soul in opposite directions. The more the wheel was turned, the more the person was stretched.

I've heard some say that the first few years of their marriage were like being on the rack. They were pulled and stretched every which way. It was painful. It was torture. At least that's the way they experienced it. But if we didn't marry, just think of the opportunity that would be lost for growth! (That's the best way to look at it. Otherwise you may end up fighting the process for years!)

People should not consider marriage unless they can accept the fact that they're not a finished product. They haven't arrived. They will need to change more than they realize or want. The person who says they don't need to change, or won't change, has a serious character defect. It's called *pride!*

Once you accept the fact that change is going to be a part of your life, you can handle it by developing an attitude that will allow you to grow. I think the attitude we need here is the same attitude that helps us deal with the adversities and sudden, unwanted upsets of life. The principle is found in James. "Consider it all joy, my brethren, when you encounter various trials, knowing that the testing of your faith produces endurance" (Jas. 1:2,3, *NASB*).

The phrase "consider it all joy" refers to an internal attitude of the heart and mind that allows us to see the long-range benefits of the trials and circumstances of life. Another way this might be translated is, "Make up your mind to regard adversity as something to welcome or be glad about." You have the power to decide what your attitude will be.

The verb tense of the word "consider" here indicates decisiveness of action. It's not an attitude of resignation like, "Oh nuts! I'm just stuck with this. That's the way life is." No, the verb tense indicates you will have to go against your natural inclination, which is to see the trial as something negative.

We need to have this attitude toward growth and change in a

marriage. If you see change as normal, desirable, not a threat, even as a challenge, you'll be all right. And you can develop such an attitude. Remind yourself that change *adds* to your life rather than takes away. You will be more motivated and more fulfilled.

Colonizers and Immigrants

In a relationship, and especially when you marry, it's as though you connect with a foreigner who has his or her own culture, set of customs and language. Think about the two kinds of travelers who visit foreign countries—the colonizer and the immigrant. A colonizer wants to visit another country to experience it from his own perspective instead of from the inhabitants' point of view. Upon entering the country, he looks for signs in his own language and seeks out people who speak his language, not even attempting to learn even the basics of the native language. He looks for the familiar and doesn't really venture into uncharted territory.

The colonizer is totally dependent upon other people from his own country who can guide him around and interpret for him. Even after he's been there for months, he doesn't get very far when he interacts with local residents. They're puzzled by what he says, and he can't comprehend them, either. It's not a happy experience for either the residents or the colonizer.

An immigrant is a different kind of person. He is somewhat of an adventurer. He actually prepares for the trip to a foreign country by orienting himself to it. He reads books about the culture and customs, the history and the food of this new land. He even attempts to learn everyday phrases of the language. In order to be able to converse with the residents, he may even take a class in their language before he begins his journey.

When an immigrant arrives at his destination, he is eager to discover all that he can. He searches out historical sites, tries all the new foods, reads as much as he can in the language of the country, and hones his verbal skills by attempting to converse in the local language whenever possible. He may even enjoy living with a family of that country for a while in order to fully capture the flavor of this new world.

As the immigrant attempts to speak this new language, the people respond in a helpful manner. They help him pronounce strange words. Often, if they are at all adept in the traveler's lan-

≈ Working together to achieve compatibility is the ultimate educational experience! ≈

guage, they will begin to speak it to make him more comfortable. Thus, they perfect their own skills as well. They seem delighted that he has made an attempt to learn their language, and both they and the immigrant can laugh at some of his mispronunciations. The immigrant has an enjoyable time, whereas the colonizer ends up being frustrated.

For a relationship to succeed, you must become an immigrant. Each person has a choice.

Or Think of It as an Education

In a healthy relationship, as in a healthy marriage, the process of becoming compatible is a mutual education. Each of you will fluctuate between two different roles. On some occasions you will function as a giving teacher. On other occasions you will be a receptive learner. If you are open to both roles, your relationship will become stronger as you become more compatible.

What will change? Attitudes, goals, values, the way you do things. You'll even be able to bring to the forefront the less developed or less preferred side of your personality.[1] Becoming compatible is therefore the ultimate educational experience.

As you become more serious in a relationship and move toward marriage, keep this in mind: You are not a finished product set in concrete and steel by what you have experienced so far in life. As one man put it, we are "potentials in the present."[2]

Actually, a marriage at any age, whether 20, 35 or 50, is a journey into a new phase of life. Look at yourself in the mirror right now. What will you be, do, think or feel 10 years from now? You see, what happens now will be harvested then.

In a marriage (I'm assuming you're interested in such a state or you wouldn't be reading this book) you will purposely or unconsciously incorporate beliefs, ideas, attitudes, values and behaviors from the other person. My wife and I still, after 38 years of marriage, surprise one another by doing something that is more like what the other person usually does than what we would assume we ourselves would choose. And when we comment on it, the other says, "Well, after living with you all these years, it was bound to rub off." You learn how to accommodate the other person, resolve problems together, modify the intensity at which you do things if it's overwhelming to your partner, and learn to rely upon your partner in a healthy way. You each want to be a helpful, positive teacher to the other.[3]

Other Insights on Compatibility

In this context of learning to complement one another in the journey of compatibility, I've always liked what Mel Krantzer says about marital love:

> Marital love requires the ability to put yourself in your partner's place, to understand that the differences that divide you are the differences of two unique personalities, rather than betrayals of your hopes and dreams. The unconditional willingness of each of you to understand and resolve these differences through the sharing of your deepest feelings, concerns, attitudes and ideas is a fundamental component of marital love.
>
> Postponement of your need for instant gratification when your partner feels no such need; sharing the struggle to triumph over adversities as well as sharing the joys and delights of being together; nurturing each other in

defeat caused by forces beyond your control and renewing each other's courage to prevail in the face of despair; carrying necessary obligations and responsibilities as a flower rather than as a hundred-pound knapsack; acknowledging the everyday value of your partner in a look, a smile, a touch of the hand, a voiced appreciation of a meal or a new hair style, a spontaneous trip to a movie or restaurant; trusting your partner always to be there when needed; knowing that he or she always has your best interests at heart even when criticism is given; loyalty and dedication to each other in the face of sacrifices that may have to be made—all of these are additional components of marital love that courtship knows little about.[4]

Scripture has some important insights about compatibility, too:

And let the peace of Christ rule in your hearts, to which indeed you were called in one body; and be thankful (Col. 3:15, NASB).

Finally, brethren, farewell (rejoice)! Be strengthened (perfected, completed, made what you ought to be); be encouraged and consoled and comforted; be of the same [agreeable] mind one with another; live in peace, and [then] the God of love [Who is the Source of affection, goodwill, love and benevolence toward men] and the Author and Promoter of peace will be with you (2 Cor. 13:11, Amp.).

So let us then definitely aim for and eagerly pursue what makes for harmony and for mutual upbuilding (edification and development) of one another (Rom. 14:19, Amp.).

Walk...with complete lowliness of mind (humility) and meekness (unselfishness, gentleness, mildness), with patience, bearing with one another and making allowances because you love one another (Eph. 4:1,2, Amp.).

Compatibility and Your Own Relationship

What does compatibility mean to you, and what does it mean for your relationship? Do you see you and your partner as compatible? Is it easier to become compatible if you and your partner are similar or different? After all, don't opposites attract? Here are some facts to remember about compatibility:

1. **Your relationship will be a blend of both similarities and differences.**
Consider what happened to Tony and Jackie as they struggled with differences in their relationship. It was a simple issue of time and order.

> In regard to the issue of time, Tony grew up in a very strict and rigid home. In his family the message regarding time was, "If you're not ten minutes early, you're late. And there is *no* excuse for being late." In his home he had the "20-to-1" rule for curfew. He had a very specific curfew and for every minute he was late, he had to be in 20 minutes earlier the following time he went out. Tony recalled having been grounded many times for being late for supper or a family outing. So time was a very big factor in his family.
>
> In regard to the issue of order, Tony describes his home this way: "I could have functioned perfectly well in my home if I had been blind. Everything had its place, and everything had better be in its place! My parents liked consistency, and they ran their home that way." Tony's father was one of those men who had pegboard up in the garage and all of the tools outlined in black marker, so you could immediately tell where a specific tool went or if one was missing. Order was also a very big factor in his family.
>
> Things were *quite* different around Jackie's house. Jackie came from what some people might call a "laid-back" family. Others might term it "chaotic." Neither time nor order were all that important in this family. The "fam-

ily rule" regarding time was somewhat of a joke both in and out of the family system: "If you're an hour either way, you're okay." It was not uncommon to hear the mother or father, when asked about the timing of something, reply, "We'll get there when we get there." Or, "It will happen when it happens!"

Tony recalls going to dinner at Jackie's house before they were married and offering to help with dishes after dinner. Having dried a platter, he asked Jackie's mom, "Where should I put this?" She gave him a puzzled look, smiled, shrugged, pointed at a cupboard and said, "Wherever there's room." In this household, car keys, checkbooks, school materials and business papers were lost on a regular basis, and there was always a last-minute, helter-skelter rush on the part of the family members to find something before they left the house. It was evident that time and order were not among the priorities of this family.

How then, out of all of the millions of people in the world, did Tony and Jackie get together? What was the attraction that would draw them toward one another despite such clear and drastic differences?

That's exactly what drew Tony and Jackie together—the *differences*. The old adage is true that opposites attract, but let's examine that principle and find out why it so often doesn't work. When Jackie became involved with Tony and got to know his family, her initial thought was, "Whew, *finally*, some structure in my life. After having grown up with all the chaos, this is great—a family that has some structure in it. At last, something I can depend on."

When Tony became involved with and got to know Jackie's family, his initial thought was, "Whew, *finally*, some laid-back people in my life. After having grown up with all that anal-retentive rigidity, this is great—a family that has some flexibility in it. At last, a place to relax."

Tony and Jackie were attracted to one another and to

each other's families based on traits that the other had, that they each *did not* have. But, what they failed to realize is very important.

They didn't have those traits for a very important reason. They couldn't tolerate them!

It was the very things that had drawn them together that were making them crazy! Tony had not yet learned that if he wanted more flexibility in his life, he had to learn how to incorporate it into his life—to create it for himself. He had to learn to identify what the messages regarding time and order were in his family of origin, determine that these would not work for him, and be prepared to commit a conscious act of disloyalty (in healthy and appropriate ways) that would help him achieve flexibility. He couldn't get it from Jackie!

Jackie had not learned that if she wanted more structure in her life, she had to learn how to incorporate it into *her* life; to create it for herself. She also had to learn to figure out what messages she had received in her family of origin regarding structure, determine that these were not helpful to her at this point in her life, create a new message that would promote healthy interactions in her marriage, and be prepared to commit that same conscious act of disloyalty to the family of origin that would help her achieve structure. She couldn't get it from Tony. Both were looking to the other to *complete* them, provide for them a trait or traits that they themselves did not have. Both had to learn that *completion comes from within— not from without!*[5]

2. **The most stable marriages are those that involve two people with many similarities.**

Dr. Neal Warren has written:

For couples, similarities are like money in the bank, and differences are like debts they owe. Suppose you received two bank statements in the mail today, one showing the amount of money in your savings account, the other showing the amount you owe on your credit card. If you

≈ Similarities can be points of conflict. So don't assume your similarities mean you don't have to work at the relationship.≈

have a large savings account and little debt, you're in a position of strength and you can weather economic storms. If a financial crisis arises, you have the means to handle it. You can make decisions and purchases without scrambling to figure out how you'll manage.

But the reverse is also true. With big debts and little savings, you're on shaky financial ground. You have to work a lot harder to cover the bills, and you worry about job security and making ends meet.

If you want to make a marriage work with someone who is very different from you, you had better have a large number of similarities as permanent equity in your account. If you don't, your relationship could be bankrupt at a frighteningly early stage.[6]

3. **Even if you have many similarities, you will still have to work at blending or meshing.**
Compatibility doesn't just happen. Your similarities could be points of conflict. So don't assume that similarities mean no work. There are always adjustments to be made and work to be done.

4. **If you are very dissimilar, you may assume that you will be the exception and will work it out.**
Just be prepared to work. You could be the exception to the exception!

5. People do tend to be attracted to an opposite quality,
    interest or behavior in a relationship.
Just remember that such opposites also have the potential to
drive you up the wall later.

6. Personally, I believe that personality differences or
    preferences have the potential for generating tremen-
    dous growth for both individuals.
Your opposite can actually help to round out your personality.
But we'll come back to this later.

Crucial Areas of Compatibility

Even though some opposites attract, compatibility still requires
similarity in certain key areas. What similarities are crucial for
compatibility?

Brain Power
One key area is a couple's intelligence. The greater the extremes
here, the greater the potential for tension. Intelligence is different from level of education. Many compatible partners have differences in their levels of schooling, but they can still relate to
each other harmoniously as long as both continue to learn and
grow—both in their own areas of interest and expertise as well
as their partner's.

A marriage can be benefited by mutual contributions in this
arena. I've seen couples in which one had a graduate-level education and the other only graduated from high school, yet they
still have a very complementary marriage. They have accepted
each other's differences and are not threatened by them. Both
persons continue to grow. But remember, for some this could be
a problem because they make it a problem. If it's important to
you that the other person have a similar level of education, don't
become involved with those who don't.

This matter of continuing to grow intellectually after marriage is one of the conflictual areas that often emerges. I have

seen so many cases where one person reads, listens to tapes, or attends seminars and classes, but her spouse is not interested in growing intellectually. Instead of moving closer together, the compatibility gap widens. One stagnates while the other grows. One may read the newspaper and her favorite novels, but does nothing to improve her mind.

I've seen this often in the area of parenting. A mother will read, attend classes and grow in her parenting skills. Although she becomes much more knowledgeable than her husband, he will tend to override her suggestions and decisions because he is the husband. I've heard such men say, "My parents did an okay job and I'm doing all right, too." Unfortunately, pride and ignorance contribute very little to wise parenting—especially in light of the fact that Scripture places more responsibility upon the role of the father than the mother.

Faith and Values

It's important that you have similar values. This can include anything from family values to spiritual values. When they are different, you have more possibility of two things happening. You face another potential area of conflict that can *drive you apart*, as well as missing one of the connecting links that can *draw you together.*

Just because both of you are Christians doesn't mean you are compatible in this area. Even if you belong to the same church, have similar tastes in worship, both have devotional lives, are knowledgeable about the Scriptures, and have the same spiritual gifts, etc., you may not be *connected.*

Values involve what is important to you. Prior to a relationship becoming serious, it is important to identify not only what your values are, but which ones you would not be willing to compromise and which ones you would. Although you may not consider certain values to be crucial, they may be to your partner.

One couple found themselves at an impasse in this area. The man had been raised in a military family and had experienced 15 moves by the time he was 20. Now, at age 27, he wanted to marry, settle down and stay in one place as a school teacher in a small town. His girl friend, however, had grown up in a small community, disliked that environment, and wanted to travel extensively as well as experience living in different areas of our country. Their relationship eventually dissolved.

Another couple had a conflict over dogs. She had been raised with them, owned two, and always wanted to have at least one or two. He did not care for dogs, and wanted her to get rid of hers before they married. (I had to admit I wasn't very objective here because I'm a dog lover with two golden retrievers.)

Negotiation and some creative alternatives have to be found in such situations, or else one partner will feel controlled and dominated by the other. This is a quick track to killing all feelings of love.

Commitment to Christ

To have a basis for compatibility both parties need to have a commitment to Christ as Lord and Savior. (See Concluding Thoughts in this book for a guide to measuring this compatibility.) It helps to have a similar view of biblical authority. How would it work if one believes that Scripture must be the final authority for what we do and think, whereas the other believes it's a guide but not the authority?

It helps if there is a similar understanding of biblical values that are important to family life. And it is vital that both partners desire to continue growing in Christ.

What about biblical roles? What do each of you believe about this issue and the concept of submission? There can be considerable discussion over this today. But regardless of the various issues in this spiritual area, I think Blaine Smith has the best statement about what is needed: "The vital matter is that each be intent upon following and growing in Christ and upon being a redemptive spiritual companion to the other."[7]

Verbal and Emotional Intimacy

It's important that you share the value of developing verbal and emotional intimacy. If there is a severe lack of this in your relationship and/or no desire on the part of one to see this grow, you're setting yourself up to be a "married single."[8]

Dr. David Augsburger had an interesting perspective on this issue of differences and similarities:

> I've heard them all—questions, complaints, pleas for help. For years people have asked me the question, "When you marry, do you end up marrying someone who is your opposite or someone who is similar?"
>
> My answer is, "Yes." I'm not copping out by saying that, because the answer is yes. It's both. There will be some similarities as well as opposites, and you have to learn to adjust to both. Think of it like this:
>
> We marry for our similarities.
>
> We stay together for our differences.
>
> Similarities satiate, differences attract.
>
> Differences are rarely the cause of conflict in a marriage. The problems arise from our similarities. Differences are the occasion, similarities are the cause.
>
> The differences may serve as the triggering event, as the issue for debate of the beef for our hassle, but it's the similarities that create the conflict between us.
>
> The very same differences that initially drew us together, later press us apart and, still later, may draw us near again. Differences first attract, then irritate, then frustrate, then illuminate and finally may unite us. Those traits that intrigue in courtship, amuse in early marriage, begin to chafe in time and infuriate in the conflicts of middle marriage; but maturation begins to change their meaning, and the uniqueness of the other person becomes prized, even in the very differences that were primary irritants.[9]

Dr. Neal Warren suggests a list of 50 items for both partners to consider and to discuss prior to marriage. Which of these have you thought about?

1. Socioeconomic background of family
2. Intelligence
3. Formal education
4. Verbal skills
5. Expected roles for both persons within the marriage
6. Views about power distribution within the family
7. Desired number of children
8. When a family should be started
9. Child-rearing views
10. Political philosophy
11. Views about smoking, alcohol and drugs
12. Amount of involvement with in-laws
13. Sense of humor
14. Punctuality
15. Dependability
16. Desire for verbal intimacy and ability to be intimate
17. The role of conflict and how to resolve it
18. The way to handle anger
19. How friendships with the opposite sex should be handled
20. Expected amount of privacy and rules for its use
21. Level of ambition
22. Life goals
23. Attitudes about weight
24. Religious and spiritual beliefs and preferences
25. Amount of church involvement
26. Family spiritual involvement
27. Hobbies and interests
28. Type of music enjoyed
29. Energy level for physical activities
30. Sexual drive and sexual interests
31. Amount of income to be spent and saved
32. How money should be allocated (clothes, vacations, etc.)
33. Amount of money to be given away and to whom
34. Degree of risks to be taken with investments
35. Attitudes about cleanliness—house, clothes, body, etc.
36. Ways of handling sickness

37. Health standards—when to see a doctor
38. Interpersonal and social skills
39. Amount and type of social involvement preferred
40. Geographical area in which to live
41. Size and style of house
42. Type of furniture and decorations
43. Amount and type of travel preferred
44. How to spend vacations
45. How to celebrate major holidays
46. How much time to spend together
47. When to go to sleep and get up
48. Temperature of home during the day and night
49. Activity during meals (talking, watching TV, etc.)
50. Television programs preferred[10]

If you're in a relationship right now, how well do you know what your partner knows, thinks or does about each of these 50 items? How well does the other know what you believe, think or do regarding these items? Isn't it time to discover this before going any further?

Notes

1. Jeanette C. Lauer and Robert H. Lauer, *Till Death Do Us Part* (New York: Harrington Park Press, 1956), pp. 157, 158. Adapted.
2. Mel Krantzer, *Creative Marriage* (New York: McGraw-Hill Co., 1981), p. 56.
3. Ibid.
4. Ibid., p. 54.
5. Dr. David Beighley, *Dancing with Yesterday's Shadows* (Muskegon, Mich.: Gospel Films Publications, 1997), pp. 68-70.
6. Neal Clark Warren, *Finding the Love of Your Life* (Colorado Springs: Focus on the Family, 1992), pp. 49, 50.
7. M. Blaine Smith, *Should I Get Married?* (Downers Grove, Ill.: InterVarsity Press, 1990), pp. 110-116. Adapted.
8. Warren, op. cit., pp. 51-54. Adapted.
9. David Augsburger, *Sustaining Love* (Ventura, Calif.: Regal Books, 1988), p. 40.
10. Warren, op. cit., pp. 60, 61.

How Different Can You Be?

≈

Differences in age, cultural upbringing, racial backgrounds and personal habits can serve as growth experiences—or as rocks that can sink your relationship.

Since we've talked about compatibility, let's get specific and meddle. Consider three significant issues in compatibility as an example of the adjustment process that a couple may face.

First of all, there is age. There is no set or right age for marriage. But there are factors which most people never bother to consider. Marrying too young brings with it minimum resources with which to handle the challenges of a marriage. Formal education is usually incomplete, as is the process of separating from parents. Life experience is limited, as are our financial resources. Many young people have never considered the ongoing challenges of marriage, let alone parenthood.

On the other end of the scale, more and more people in our society don't marry until their 30s. There are many pluses to this.

Usually the individuals are established occupationally, education is complete, they have lived on their own, and they have had numerous life experiences.

The downside is that there is a greater likelihood you are set in your ways if you have lived for several years as a single person. A man may have already purchased a home, furnished it according to standards based on *his* evaluation of consumer research reports. When his bride comes into his home, instead of neutral territory in which she has the freedom to express her individuality, she may meet with incredible resistance. Each partner will have established their living, cooking, financial and recreational patterns.

Of course it's not impossible for such marriages to work. I've seen them work. You just need to be aware of this challenge ahead of time. The attempt to integrate someone else into your life after you have reached some maturity will require patience, understanding and flexibility—and an ability to see life through another's eyes. Over the past decade I've been involved in the premarital preparation of numerous couples in their 30s and 40s, as well as several age-different couples including a 35- and 22-year-old, 41 and 22, 41 and 27, and 41 and 24.

More About Age Differences

It's interesting to consider the beliefs we hold concerning age differences between a man and woman. When you read about the four couples I just cited, you thought the older one in each case was the male, didn't you? Go ahead, you can admit it. I would have. And in those cases, you're right. But there have been numerous others in which the age difference was just the reverse, with the woman being considerably older than the man.

Isn't it interesting that we have a different level of acceptance and understanding when it's the man who is older rather than the woman? Why *is* that? What are your beliefs in this area? I've heard some say it's not so much the chronological age difference but the emotional maturity. I remember a 38-year-old man marrying a 24-year-old woman who told me they were very well matched because he was closer to 28 emotionally and his fiancée was much more mature than her years.

I've heard younger women (late 20s and early 30s) say they preferred men in their 40s rather than their own age group because of the difference in maturity. As one woman said, "Actually, men my age bore me. Most of them have not developed emotionally and some are hanging on as long as they can to some part of their adolescence."

Men in their 40s have normally experienced their midlife transition (which is not the same as a midlife crisis) and have evaluated where they've been, where they are, where they want to go and what their values are. Many are no longer in pursuit of building their identity through their work, but rather are much more interested in intimacy and relationships. *This* is the factor that is attracting the younger women to them. And there is something to be said for this.

There is a rule of thumb to consider here. A few years' difference doesn't make much of a difference. However, when the difference is 10 or 15 or 20 years, the adjustment and potential problem index rises accordingly. I still wish we could somehow find a way to measure emotional and social age differences.

I was raised in a home with significant age differences. When I was born, my mother was 37 and my dad was 49. My friends asked me what it was like to have "old" parents. I couldn't understand what they meant because to me they didn't seem old. As I look back now I see some of the issues they had to deal with as older parents, as well as issues that arose from their age difference. But they had a common bond of both being hard workers. They lived (and I was born) during a survival phase in our society that included the Great Depression and World War II. The culture was more other-centered and family-centered than it is today. My parents made it work. Many today don't.

It does appear that age differences are not as significant when both are older. If one is 22 and the other 37, there are differences in terms of social interests, financial purposes, sexual drive, etc. If the 22-year-old is a woman, when her sexual responsiveness is peaking in her early 30s, her husband's may have plateaued and even diminished. At 22 she may not be as interested in saving for retirement as he is, but would rather spend and enjoy.

On the other hand, if the woman is 48 and the man 63, both have had a multitude of experiences in life to mold them. Their reasons for marriage could be a bit different than at 22 and 37. And keep in mind that one or both could come with a package deal—children. That is often a significant cause of a second marriage ending in divorce.

Some of the problems inherent in age differences include impatience with the younger spouse; a tendency to parent, to want to hold onto "your" money, to engage in power struggles; and resistance to giving up some of your friends and/or activities for the sake of the relationship.

Perhaps none of these are problems or issues for you, but they are for many.[1]

We Marry Foreigners

One of the challenges facing every couple is the fact that when you marry you are marrying a foreigner. It's true. We all marry a foreigner. My daughter did. Sheryl is a mixture of English, French, German and Native American. And who did she marry? A man who is Irish and Scottish. But it really wasn't an issue since both are eighth- or tenth-generation Americans.

They both reflect the culture they share in common for the most part, although Bill really likes his Irish heritage. He's even learned some of the Gælic language and customs. The only problem we've encountered with it is with his dog Kushanea—that's Gælic for "Fire Dog." (Bill named him that because he's a firefighter.) Bill and Sheryl decided to train their dog. That was great. But they decided to teach him the commands in Gælic, and that wasn't so great! No one else can tell that dog what to do because he isn't bilingual. So when he comes to visit we have a 140-pound Irish (what else?) wolfhound prancing through our house totally ignoring us. So much for Gælic!

You marry a foreigner in the sense that each home we come from has its own little mini-culture which most of us tend to believe is the best. You and your partner may have been raised in the same city and the same neighborhood. You may have attended the same school and/or church. Yet there will still be some significant cultural differences that need clarification. These "small cultural differences" often are very evident when it comes to planning the wedding. The potential for conflict is overwhelming.

Remember that your own mini-culture is like the lens of a camera that shapes and colors how you respond to conflict and how you interpret what occurs. Each of you could see the same event in a different way because of your background.

In one of the graduate classes I taught I learned about the significance of cultures within a culture. Many cultures were represented in the class, including a number of Korean and Chinese students. In each cultural group some were first-generation, some second and some third. There was a striking contrast between the first generation—who were very traditional and whose primary language was their native tongue—and the third generation, who were very Americanized.

One Chinese girl who was third-generation made a fascinating comment. She said, "I would be interested in James (his American name). He's very bright and good-looking, but we would never get along. He's too Chinese for me."

I've seen these differences apparent in other groups as well. The first generations are settled in their original culture, whereas members of the second generation are beginning to venture into a new culture. Third and fourth generations are the transitional groups and are often more eager to move forward than to maintain their roots.

Interracial Differences
Interracial relationships are becoming more and more common. In such cases, various factors that contribute to the challenge of compatibility should be considered.

Values are very important because they tend to infuse many of the other issues involved in an interracial marriage. A value reflects what is important to a person and what he or she may see as good or bad, right or wrong, important or unimportant. Values can be reflected in morals, dress, religion, food and the way one behaves in public or when guests are entertained.

Food is an issue for many. Not only the type of food or the way it is cooked and eaten, but many other factors emerge as well. Consider these cultural differences. A Chinese wife may use her own chopsticks to pass and serve food to family members and guests. For her, this is a way of showing respect, kindness and intimacy. But to her Japanese husband, this is dirty and disrespectful. In his own culture a person uses his own chopsticks and his own bowl. In a Japanese funeral ceremony the chopsticks are used to transfer the bones of the dead from the monk to the family member. The emotional involvement in these conflicting customs can easily override the intellectual understanding of the differences.

The Irish drink at wakes, the Japanese have ritual tea ceremonies, and Jewish sons express love to their mothers through the extent of their appetites. Food issues involve what is eaten and how it is prepared, when the main meal is served, and where and how it is eaten. Some cultures have the main meal at noon, others in the evening. Even in our country many farm people refer to lunch as dinner and the large meal is eaten at noon. This can be a major adjustment for a city person marrying a farm person.

Sex is an issue. Such things as contraception, menstruation, family honor, affection in public, hygiene, dancing, dress and holding hands in public all could be issues.

Male-female roles will often require adjustment. Much of this will have to do with the issue of male superiority, which differs from culture to culture. In some societies male dominance is subtle; in others it is blatant. In some cultures there is a blending of roles, whereas in others there are prescribed standards.

The *use of time* is yet another concern. What's considered to be late in one culture is not late in another. Some cultures are more relaxed and unhurried than our American system. Some people are used to napping after a large meal at noon. If a person marries and moves to his spouse's country, he not only has to adjust to the person but to the timetable of the land as well.

≈ The greatest problem faced by interracial couples is the matter of rearing offspring. Their children become the embodiment of their unresolved cultural differences. ≈

The greatest problem faced by interracial couples is the matter of *rearing offspring*. The children typically are considered marginal to two different cultures. They have one foot in each culture, but not enough to be distinctive. Many interracial couples have said that everything was fine between them until they had children. The child becomes the embodiment of the differences in values, family background and any other issues that the couple has been unable to resolve by the time a child arrives. The naming of the child, the way a child is handled, schooling, questions of sexuality, and so forth are involved here.

Some cultures, such as the Latin, Asian, Middle Eastern and many European societies, are much more authoritarian than others. Others, such as North American, Scandinavian and some island cultures, are more lenient and permissive. If these two different orientations mix in marriage and parenthood, there will be conflict. Punishment and discipline styles are the major conflicts that arise from child-rearing in these families. Nonetheless, children can be a bonding agent in an intercultural marriage, actually strengthening it.

Communication and language problems do not just involve the language. In the beginning of a relationship, struggles to understand the other person are accepted and even intriguing; but later they can become a major problem. In speaking different languages there is more possibility that the messages can be distorted or not fully understood. A positive word in one language may be offensive in another. A title in one language and culture may have a much different interpretation in another. The humor of one culture is not necessarily the humor of another culture.

Language can affect the balance of power in a relationship. Usually, the person speaking his own language in his own country (when his partner is not) has the advantage and power. The more fluent person has more influence.

Gestures and body language can have different meanings. Silence means different things in different cultures. Even eye contact varies. For an Arab, trust is developed through eye contact, whereas for a Japanese too much eye contact is rude and can become offensive.

The distance one stands in relationship to another person varies from culture to culture. One of my graduate students was raised in Chile and would stand about six inches away from my face when talking to me. At first, I was quite uncomfortable since my personal space had been invaded. But after he explained the difference to me and I talked to him several times, my discomfort left and I purposely would stand close to his face. I enjoyed learning to be more flexible.

In one culture being frank, blunt, demonstrative, direct, probing and aggressive are accepted. But in another such behavior is offensive because that culture values being tentative, discreet and subtle. To Asians, Americans are too loud and boisterous; but to the Arab culture, we are too reserved.

In a mixed marriage of any kind, the couple has to decide *how they express their faith*—how to celebrate holidays, maintain two sets of family traditions and handle other people's response to their relationship. Couples must decide which of these elements in their differing backgrounds are to be used to instill a sense of identity in their children.

Other adjustment areas for interracial couples may include where the couple lives, politics, friends, finances, in-laws, social class and how to deal with stress, illness and suffering. Of course these differences cited by interracial couples may be the same to some degree for any couple. But that is the difference—*degree*. For the interracial couple the differences are more pronounced, more intense, more emotionally connected. The differences are especially acute for the partner living in the native land of her spouse. She may soon begin to feel isolated, outnumbered and lonely.[2]

Examples from the Trenches

Consider these adjustment issues among several interracial couples.

Jan is an American Caucasian Christian woman engaged to a man from Greece. From his cultural perspective he is quite up-to-date and modern in his view of the equality of male-female roles. But from Jan's perspective he's a chauvinist who expects her to defer to him. When they discuss this issue, he considers his tone of voice a "bit intense, but respectful." Jan views it as yelling and verbally abusive.

Jim is an English man who is married to a Mexican-American woman from a large extended family. (Jim calls it a tribe.) He enjoys his in-laws, but he has problems with the amount of time she wants to spend with them, because from his perspective they already see the in-laws more than is "normal."

An Italian-American man is married to Sarah, a Jewish-American woman. Their conflict is over the discipline of their children. She sees her husband as being too strict, whereas he sees her letting the kids get away with murder. Sarah also feels that since her husband converted to her Jewish religion he's become a fanatic. She's culturally Jewish, which is enough for her, and she doesn't want him taking the kids to the synagogue so much.

Two black students are engaged. He's from Trinidad and has been in this country for two years. He loves the freedom and opportunities in this country and is so thankful to be here. She grew up in a New York ghetto and is angry and embittered over the racism and inequality she sees all around her. She also thinks he is naive and needs to see this country for the racist society she believes it really is.

Juanita, an Argentine-Estonian woman, fell in love with Jon, a

Norwegian-American. They worked in the same company and were highly attracted to one another. After six months they had their first conflict. The more she talked about it, expressing her feelings and trying to resolve it, the quieter he became. In fact he was just silent. For hours he would say nothing. Finally she blew up. She told him his silence was driving her crazy and making her angry.

When they discussed the problem, they made a discovery. He said that, in his family, being quiet was the way to keep the peace. He had never seen his parents quarrel. But in her family if you were upset and didn't show it, it meant you didn't care. So their way of connecting with each other was direct and often angry. Yet they were usually able to resolve issues between them.[3]

These are all issues of conflict which arose specifically over differences in culture. Although any of the issues could have impacted the relationship of couples from the same background, different cultures simply contribute more fuel for these conflicts to arise.

Couples from different cultures or races may be attracted to each other because of the excitement of cultural contrasts; but they should be aware that the same attraction can result in cultural clashes.

"Metabolic" Differences

Let's consider another set of adjustments. We call them "metabolism conflicts"—and most couples have them. Resolving them contributes to compatibility, but if they remain conflicts they act as continual irritants. Each one of the differences outlined here could come as a surprise. Even if you're aware of them, once you are married and living with these differences a different dynamic is created.

You may discover that you have different ideas about what time to go to bed, what time to get up, whether you're actually awake and functioning when you wake up or it takes two hours to get in gear, whether to sleep with the room totally dark or with a light on or a with window open or closed.

You discover that one needs strong espresso coffee in the morning and the other no coffee, but lots of fruit juice and vitamins. One works extra hours every day, whereas the other needs a nap before dinner.

One partner may go through life at a rapid pace, whereas the other moves more slowly. One young couple found this out when they visited some art museums for the first time on their honeymoon. June would keep walking and scanning as they went through, while Bob wanted to linger and soak up each picture or statue. He kept saying "slow down," whereas she urged him to keep up. They still visit museums, but once they get there they agree to browse and gaze at their own pace and to meet at a certain time. In this way they can take in 10 or 80 paintings according to their individual preferences, and both of them get what they want out of the experience.

Listen to how this couple worked out a difference in values. They learned what all couples need to learn—tolerance and acceptance of differences.

Herb is what I call a health nut. He has to work out each and every day, and he's encouraged me to do the same. I discovered that seven days a week is too hard on me, so I let him know that since only three days were enjoyable for me, that would be my limit.

The real problem arose over what we ate. He's into all this veggie stuff with bean sprouts and tofu. He was really on my case to eat his way and give up sugar, meat, etc. Some of what he said was all right, but there were a number of things I just didn't want to give up. He gave me lectures and looks of disgust when I ate something that was off his list. So we had a discussion. I let him know that I liked much of what I ate and intended to keep eating it. I didn't want or need him to be my conscience. So it seemed to work out. But as we got more serious, I wondered what we would do if we married. So I asked a few questions.

What diet would we follow if we married? If we each

had our own, would we be fixing two separate meals? What would we expect our children to eat? How would this affect friendships and eating out?

There are two possible conclusions to this story. One is that couples can decide it's too much work and hassle to try to work out something like this. There would always be a sense of tension in the air. The other is that they can learn to tolerate differences, to adjust and adapt where necessary, to discover alternatives never before considered and become stronger in the process. To become compatible, this is what it takes.

What about you? Had you thought about all of these issues and areas of possible conflict? This is the time to explore and learn.

Notes

1. Barbara DeAngelis, *Are You the One for Me?* (New York: Dell Books, 1992), pp. 218-223. Adapted.
2. Dugan Romano, *Intercultural Marriage* (Yarmouth, Maine: Intercultural Publications, 1988), pp. 64-87, 96-102. Adapted.
3. Joel Croham, *Mixed Matches* (New York: Fawcett Columbine, 1995), pp. 4, 5. Adapted.

If Men Are from Mars and Women from Venus, How on Earth Can They Communicate?

≈

*Learning to "genderflex"—to adapt to the
communication style of the opposite sex—can both
enrich your personality and save your relationship.*

Many years ago (more than I will admit to) I learned to drive a car. It was a stick shift, primarily because very few cars had automatic transmissions then. The gear shift was on the steering column. It was tricky, learning to coordinate the pushing of the clutch as you shifted from one gear to the next. If you did it right, it went smoothly and quietly. If not, you ground the gears. You could hear as well as feel the metal clashing and grinding. If you did this often enough you would grind the gears into fine pieces of metal, eventually ruining the transmission.

The same thing can happen to two people attempting to

become compatible. You can end up grinding and clashing against one another. Aside from the previously discussed areas of meshing that need to occur, another major issue comes into play when you seek to learn each other's culture. It's the blending of your gender (male/female) and personality differences.

Too often we hear gender differences reduced to one factor such as personality preferences, or being left- or right-brained. It actually makes more sense to look at men and women as a complex mixture of differences. In that way you can understand them better.

Understanding and adapting to your partner's personality—which includes gender uniqueness as well as brain dominance—will make the difference between whether you adjust to this foreigner or not! When you and your partner are in synch, the gears don't grind as you shift into a close relationship.

To make this happen, you need to accept two facts:

1. Men and women are wired differently. Neither is wired *wrong*, just differently.
2. For your relationship to blossom, you need to become a "bilingual" couple, each fluent in the language of the opposite sex.

Accepting Gender Differences

It's not easy to flex and learn to respond differently; but it's possible. What is second nature for you has to be a conscious effort on your partner's part, and vice versa.

I've heard many men and women today say they know about the differences between women such as feeling vs. fact, brain difference, energy levels, etc. But their interaction often leads me to question this. If they know it, why do they keep fighting something that is a natural and inherited ability, as well as having been designed by God Himself?

If people really knew the differences between male and female styles of thinking and communicating, then they would be able to explain the differences in detail, accept them and change the way they respond to each other. They would honor the differences and respond in an appropriate and accepting way.

The following may seem like a basic course in biology, physiology and anthropology, but it really isn't. It's simply an explanation of some basic gender differences that most people still allow to confuse them—and dictate their response to the opposite sex.

Large-Brained Girls!

We're going to start by looking at men and women as children. Let's assume we have X-ray glasses so we can look into their brains. As you peer inside, you may see a discrepancy between boys and girls.

In the brain there is a section that connects the left and right hemispheres. It's a bundle of nerves (the technical name is *corpus callosum*) and it can be up to 40 percent larger in girls than in boys. This means that women are able to use both sides of the brain together at one time, whereas men have to switch from one side of their brain to the other depending upon what they need. Women can enjoy more cross talk between the sides.

This extra connective tissue in girls is a reason why they develop language skills earlier than boys and will use many more words than the young male of our species. Do you know why boys often read more poorly than girls? It's the brain again. There's the culprit. *The brain that will read better is the brain that can use both sides of the brain at once.* Interestingly, it's also easier to "read" the emotions on a person's face when you use both sides of your brain simultaneously.

A woman's brain has been developed to express and verbalize. This is why throughout adulthood she wants to "talk about it." A man's brain has been geared to developing his spatial skills. This is why throughout his life he wants to "do something" about it. So a woman is typically quicker to talk about her feelings, while a man wants to act quickly to *do* something about it.

Of course you recognize that this is where conflicts arise (and probably always will). A woman will say, "Let's sit down and talk this through thoroughly." Meanwhile the man is straining at the bit to get it fixed and get on with life! Remember: Neither response is wrong, and neither is better than the other.

Male-Female Brain Maps

In studies at the University of Pennsylvania, brainscan equipment has been used to generate computer photographs of brains in use. They look almost like maps. The equipment photographs the brain in different colors, with each color showing a different degree of intense cortical activity.

A man and a woman are hooked up to the equipment. They are both asked to do a spatial task, figuring out how two objects fit together. If you were looking at a computer screen depicting the woman's brain, this is what you would see: In the woman's brain, the color and intensity on both sides are pretty equal. But something happens to the man's brain. The right side lights up with various colors that reflect a high degree of right-brain activity. But much less of the left hemisphere lights up.

On the other hand, when verbal skills are tested, watch out! Then you would see that the man uses much less of his brain than the woman's. (If you're a woman reader you're probably saying right now, "I knew that!") But in the woman's brain the intensity of activity in her left hemisphere really lights up!

The findings of this research indicate that a woman's brain is at work in more sections than the man's almost all the time. It's like both hemispheres are always on call, whereas in a man's brain they are not—or at least not in the same way.

Think of it like this: If there's a task to do, a man's brain turns on. When the task is completed, the brain turns off. But a woman's brain is always on. It's true that parts of a man's brain are always on, but when the two brains are compared in their downtime or inactive time, the difference between the portion of the woman's brain that's always on and a man's on/off brain is quite pronounced.[1]

So what does this difference mean? The difference is the main reason men are such fixers, so task-oriented, and not as able to do several things at once. They need to focus on one thing at a time. When a man takes on a task at home such as cleaning the garage or working in the yard, to him it's a single-focus task, *not a fellowship time.* If his wife wants to work with him, she usually wants to carry on a conversation at the same time. To him this may seem an interruption, an invasion of his space, a distraction, and he reacts strongly to it. Millions and perhaps billions of conflicts over the years could have been avoided if men and women had not only understood this but honored the difference.

Men and Emotions

This brings us to a question that I've heard again and again over the years: *Why can't men get into feelings like a woman does?* The answer is that men have three strikes against them when it comes to feelings.

One, they're wired differently.

Two, they're raised to be emotionally handicapped. They're given neither the encouragement nor training to learn to understand a wide range of feelings, nor to develop a vocabulary to express them.

Third, the way women respond to men to get to their feelings often becomes counterproductive.

Again, we must look at the brain to see why men and women have to deal with their feelings differently. A woman has an immense number of neuroconnecters between her feelings and the "broadcasting studio" in her brain. She has an expressway which runs between her feelings and her speech. And because her brain is basically on all the time, it's very easy for her to share these feelings.

On the other hand, remember that a man's brain has fewer nerve connectors between its right and left sides. No wonder, then, that he often has more of a struggle than a woman in expressing feelings. He doesn't have an expressway between feelings and the broadcasting area of the brain, but more of a one-way road.[2]

This is why it's not easy for a man to share. If he attempts to put his feelings into words, he must take a prior step called *thought.* He has to ask, "Now, I'm feeling something. What is it? All right, that's what it is." Once he discovers his feelings, he must analyze them and decide what he can do about them.

Remember that a man's brain is a problem-solving brain. He is wired to have delayed reactions. When an emotional event occurs, is he ready yet to express his feelings? No. He needs to move over to the left side of his brain and collect the words he knows that express his feelings. That's what stops many men from expressing emotions, because they are vocabulary-deficient for the most part.

≈ A man has to think about his feelings
before he can share them. A woman can feel,
talk and think at the same time. ≈

And it's not all their fault. Parents, teachers and society as a whole fail to provide much help in teaching men the vocabulary of feelings or the ability to paint word pictures to describe them. The man shares what he's able to share, and when new feelings arise, it's back to the drawing board to start the process all over again.

So remember this difference: A man has to think about his feelings before he can share them. A woman can feel, talk and think at the same time.[3]

Women and Emotions

The sequence a woman goes through is quite different. When a woman is upset, what does she do first? She talks about it. And as she talks she is able to think about what she is saying and feeling. The end result is that she figures it out, usually by herself. She begins with feelings, then moves to talking and then to thinking. Eventually she develops the ability to do all three at the same time:

| Feeling | | Talking | | Thinking |

Because a woman "problem-solves" out loud, most men either think they've caused the problem or that the woman wants them to solve the problem. It's possible that he *should* fix it, but only if she requests a solution. Most women just want their man to listen and reflect the fact that they've heard what she is saying.

Now, a man is not going to deal with his feelings in the same way because they develop in another order. Often his feelings develop, then he moves to action and then to thinking. When an upset occurs, the immediate response is to do something about it; and that helps him think it through. In time, he learns to feel, *act* and think at the same time:

| Feeling |————————| Acting |————————| Thinking |

You will notice that *talking* to resolve the problem isn't part of the formula for men. Communication is more significant for a woman, while action is more significant for a man.[4]

When a woman understands this, she doesn't have to be surprised when it occurs. She can accept it and even encourage the man to respond in this way and adapt some of her typical responses to more nearly match his.

Keep in mind that each side of the brain has, as it were, its own language. If a man is stronger in his left brain (in other words, if he's left-brain dominant) his language is going to be concerned with facts. It will be tend to be logical and precise, as well as black and white.

To Summarize "LB" Men

Let's summarize what you will hear from a typical man. We'll call him "LB" for "left brain."

The communication is precise to make sure he is understood.

The vocabulary used is very rational, and may even be authoritarian.

Logic is the basis of reference. He likes to go from 1 to 2 to 3 to 4, not from 1 to 3 to 2 to 4!

When he communicates, the purpose is to clarify.

At the heart of his communication is critical or analytical thinking.

The language he uses may seem sterile and unimaginative because it's so objective.

He asks questions in order to understand a woman's logic.

When he solves problems, he will use language to guide the woman to the "correct" solution.

Who does this describe—you or your partner? If this isn't you, how do you feel about this style of communication? If this isn't you, do you understand this style of communication?

What could you do to speak your partner's language?

A Summary of "RB" Women

If a woman's dominant side of the brain is the right side, her language will reflect this.

It will primarily be a language of feelings.

It will tend to be ambiguous.

The vocabulary she selects will tend to be empathic and emotional.

There will be an emphasis upon attachment and interdependence.

She will use metaphors and symbols rather than being precise and direct.

She will view communication to an RB (right brain) as a connecting experience.

The heart of her communication is the sharing of experiences.

She will use the subjective language of intimacy.

When she asks questions, they will be for the purpose of figuring out how experience has brought her to what she thinks and believes now.

When she problem-solves, she will function like a midwife—using language to assist others in coming to their own solution.[5]

Who does this describe—you or your partner? If this isn't you, how do you feel about this style of communication? If this isn't you, do you understand this style of communication? What could you do to speak the other person's language?

"Genderflex": Bridging the Gap

This whole business of relationships is about left-brained men and right-brained women being attracted to each other. If they are ever to communicate across their natural gender gap, if they are to develop into a functional couple, they must learn to understand and use the other person's language style to some extent. They must become "bilingual"! Can you make this switch?

The differences we have outlined between the brains of men and women mean that when they communicate (or attempt to!) they have different purposes in mind. Women speak and hear a language of connection and intimacy, whereas a man tends to speak and hear a language of status and independence.

≈ Men speak "report" talk. They like to express knowledge and skills. Women's speech is "rapport" talk. It's their way of establishing connections. ≈

The way men speak is "report talk." They like to express knowledge and skills. They use talking as a way to get and keep attention.

Women's speech is *rapport*-talk. It's their way of establishing connections and negotiating relationships.

So what you have is not really a difference of dialects within the same language, but cross-cultural communication. It's been said that men and women speak different *genderlects.*[6]

This area of difference is not just a concern in marriage but in the workplace as well:

The male-female difference represents the biggest culture gap that exists. If you can learn the skills and attitudes to bridge the gender differences in communication, you will have mastered what it takes to communicate and negotiate *with* almost anyone *about* almost anything.[7]

A new word, "genderflex," has been coined for this situation. It's not in any dictionary yet, but it will be. The word means to temporarily use communication patterns typical of the other gender in order to connect with them and increase the potential for influence.[8]

This is an adaptive approach to communication designed to improve relationships and performance. It's not a change in personality, lifestyle or values. It's an adaptation that will actually create greater flexibility and growth among those practicing it. You choose to communicate in the patterns of the other gender to accomplish a goal. You simply adopt the characteristics of the other's gender that are related to style, content and structure of communication. You're not becoming like the other gender, but showing that you understand how they communicate.

"Genderflex" talk will remember that women tend to speak the language of "expressers" and men the language of "resolvers." A simple example of this is that typically most women are "expanders" and most men are "condensers" in the content of what they share. That is, women tend to give much more detail and include feelings in what they share, whereas men tend to give bottom-line, factual information. So to speak the other person's language, even if a woman were talking about interpersonal situations, she would use more factual descriptions that focus on identifying a problem or a solution rather than an abundance of details or feelings. And a man would not give just "bottom-line" facts but descriptive details with an emphasis on the interpersonal.[9]

Keep in mind that you will find exceptions to these male-female styles. Some men will express themselves as RB's, and some women will come across as LB's. Personally I think this is due to the influence of personality variation.

By the way, are you aware that men talk more than women? It's true! There hasn't been a single study that gives any evidence that women talk more than men, but there are numerous studies showing that men talk more than women. Each simply talk about their preferred topics.[10]

I've heard both men and women say, "Why should I go to all this work of adapting and changing? If my partner would talk less (or talk more) and listen, everything would be all right."

My response has always been, "Is what you are doing to help the situation working?"

I know what I'll hear. "No."

"Then why keep doing it? There's a better way."

A Message to Men

What can a man do to help bridge the communication gap between genders? What if he has never learned to share his feelings, or in other ways to "genderflex" or adapt to the language of women? Several basic steps can make a difference.

First, never compare your verbal agility with a woman's ability to share. Such a comparison may keep you from trying. Listening to some women speak so freely of the feelings dimension of life may cause you to think, *Forget it, I couldn't share like that, nor do I want to!* No one is suggesting that you share the way a woman does. But you *can* develop your untapped potential for expressing unmasked feelings and developing intimacy.

Second, realize that becoming aware of and sharing your feelings offers you a multitude of life-changing benefits. It brings you closer to God's intended plan for your life. As a result, you will relate significantly better to a wider range of people, including feelings-oriented men and women. More people will listen to you and respond to you.

Third, listen to how others describe and share their feelings. Learn from them. Make a list of feeling words and memorize them. Expand other areas of your vocabulary as well, and use these new terms in sentences within your mind until you become comfortable with them. Some men I know have practiced out loud to accustom themselves to hearing the spoken words.

Fourth, learn to use word pictures to describe what is going on inside yourself. Instead of just saying, "I had a hard day," you could describe your day like this: "At times today it was so rough and frustrating I felt like I was trying to push an elephant out of the way and it finally sat on me!" Or, "At one point today it seemed like it was raining on everything I tried. I was really discouraged."

Fifth, try writing out what is going on inside you. If you have a habit of saying "I think," you could change it to "I feel" or "I felt" or "My inner reaction was...." Practice, pray, and believe that God can work in your emotional life.

Sixth, let the woman in your life know that one of your goals is to learn to share your feelings with her, and tell her you need her help and support. The following suggestions will alleviate misunderstandings and help to enlist the support you need:

1. Explain that it will be difficult for you, and that it would be helpful to you if she recognized your progress.

2. Let her know that sometimes the way you share may not seem clear and may differ from the way she would share in response to the same experience. Let her know that you want to understand. Tell her it would be best if she just asked a simple clarifying question rather than trying to correct what you say or the way you say it.

3. Give yourself permission to process your thoughts. There will be times when you need first to think through what you are feeling to access your emotions. If there is silence, don't fill it in with words or questions.

4. Ask for understanding and grace. Tell her that when feelings are shared, you don't want to hear judgments, criticisms or interruptions.

5. Ask for confidentiality when personal feelings are shared. Let her know that you would prefer that these not be shared with others.

6. State clearly what you want. If you don't want to *discuss* your feelings but simply *state* them, let her know that, too. She is not a mind-reader.

7. When your partner wants to discuss her feelings, find a time that is agreeable for both of you. Look at her, listen and reflect her feelings by asking questions and clarifying what you heard. Don't take what she says as a personal attack, and don't try to fix her.

Stu Weber, writing in his book to men, *Tender Warrior*, had this message for all men:

Women speak a different language than men. It's not Spanish or Korean or Swahili. It's not Hindi or Hebrew. It's "Woman," and it's spoken all over the planet. Yes, I suppose men have a language of sorts, too, but that's not the issue here. The crux of the matter is that women speak their own unique dialect and it is incumbent upon Tender

Warriors to learn that language and speak it with passion.

I'm reminded of a cross-cultural snapshot one of my friends described to me. On a brief trip to Haiti, he found himself alone in a room with a young Haitian man who seemed wide-eyed with excitement about meeting an American. The Haitian obviously longed to open a conversation. His hands opened and closed. His eyes burned with a desire to weave his thoughts into understandable words. He seemed to have a thousand questions on the tip of his tongue. But my friend didn't speak a word of Creole and the Haitian didn't speak English. So eventually, after a few smiles, nods, vague gestures and self-conscious shrugs, the two young men strolled awkwardly to different corners of the room, and they parted—almost certainly for the rest of their lives.

That little experience paints a powerful analogy in my mind. You and I know men and women who live together 10, 20, 50 years or more but never learn to speak one another's language. They sit in rooms together, ride in cars together, eat meals together, take vacations together and sleep together when the sun goes down. But for year after year they never learned how to get beyond vague gestures and a few surface phrases.

That, my friend, is a *man's* responsibility. He is the one who must take the initiative and learn how to speak "Woman." There it is in clear terms.

In 1 Peter 3:7 it says, "You husbands...live with your wives in an understanding way, as with a weaker vessel, since she is a woman; and grant her honor as a fellow heir of the grace of life."

Webster defines understanding as "gaining a full mental grasp." Not bad. Those are words we men ought to be able to grapple with. To understand is to gain a full mental grasp of the nature and significance of something. To understand is a mental process of arriving at a result. It's when you study and study an issue, turn it this way and that, and suddenly the wires connect, the light blinks on and you say, "Ah-ha! So *that's* the way it works!" There ought to be ah-ha's as we seek to comprehend the implications of womanhood. Men are commanded to understand, to comprehend, to apprehend the meaning of, to grasp the force of living with a woman. Understanding involves a discerning skill, a rational process and a reasoned judgment.[11]

A Word to the Women

What is the best way for a woman to express her emotions to a man, especially if he has difficulty coping with feelings?

1. Plan ahead and practice whenever possible. Share your feelings in small increments, piecemeal; don't dump them all at once. Emotional overloading tends to short-circuit and overwhelm men.
2. Ask a man, "What is your reaction?" rather than, "What are you feeling?"
3. Think of communicating with a man as speaking your native language to someone from another culture. I have learned to do this with my Asian students, and they appreciate it.
4. Above all, never interrupt him when he's sharing. Be patient. It will take him longer than you to process his thoughts and feelings and express himself.

As we have said, not all men and women fit these descriptions. There are many exceptions and variations. That's why we need to avoid stereotypes of men and women. Both men and women may have characteristics typical to their gender in some ways, but be different in others.

My wife Joyce and I are examples. She is very single-minded, and needs to focus on one task at a time. Handling several things at one time is not her forte. On the other hand, I tend to be the juggler, handling several things at once. Through testing I've discovered that I'm neither right- nor left-brain dominant. They are both the same.

When you see such variations or exceptions in your partner, don't classify them as odd or wrong. Just be aware that they exist, and adapt your own communication style accordingly.

Notes

1. Michael Gurian, *The Wonder of Boys* (New York: G. P. Putnam, 1996), pp. 11-15. Adapted.
2. Ibid., p. 23. Adapted.
3. John Gray, *What Your Mother Couldn't Tell You and Your Father Didn't Know* (New York: HarperCollins, 1994), p. 90, adapted; and Joe Tanenbaum, *Male & Female Realities* (San Marcos, Calif.: Robert Erdmann Publishing, 1990), chaps. 4-6, adapted. See also Gray's book, *Mars and Venus Together Forever*, and his even more popular *Men Are from Mars and Women Are from Venus*, also from HarperCollins.
4. Gray, op. cit., pp. 90-91. Adapted.
5. Rebecca Cutter, *When Opposites Attract* (New York: Dutton Publishing, 1994), pp. 43, 44. Adapted.
6. Deborah Tannen, Ph.D., *You Just Don't Understand* (New York: Morrow Publishing, 1990), pp. 42, 77. Adapted.
7. See *Transcultural Leadership, Empowering the Diverse Work Force* (Houston, Tex.: Gulf Publishing, 1993).
8. Judith C. Tingley, Ph.D., *Genderflex* (New York: Amacom, 1993), p. 16. Adapted.
9. Ibid., p. 19. Adapted.
10. Ibid., p. 29. Adapted.
11. Stu Weber, *Tender Warrior* (Sisters, Oreg.: Multnomah Books, 1993), pp. 119-121.

Personality Types: People Who Need People vs. Private Persons

≈

It helps to be aware of your personality type,
but don't envy someone else's to the point that you
apologize for who you are. God created all types,
so it's all right to be you!

Now that we've looked at some of the differences between men and women and their communication styles, you may be saying, "But not all men are alike! Not really. Some guys I know are so different from other men. Why is that, and how do I talk to *them*? When I meet someone new, how do I figure out the best way to talk to *him*?"

Or you may be asking the same questions about women. And these are good questions.

Differences in personality types are the reason you see such variations among people. Through the years, several models have been developed to explain differences in personality. They all have their strengths. The one that I have discovered to be most helpful is based on the Myers-Briggs Type Indicator (MBTI).

I have seen conflicted couples married for 20 years or more become loving, compatible, growing couples after they discovered their individual uniqueness based on the MBTI. Both in counseling and in seminars I've seen relationships change for the better once a person understood his personality, his partner's, the fact that it's all right for each of them to be the way they are, and then how to adapt to one another.

Remember: In developing a relationship you need to be who you are—don't downplay your personality. Sometimes people think, *If I'm really me they won't like me, so I'll mellow out.* This is courtship deception.

As we look at these personality types remember that this is the way you were uniquely created. It's your bent, your inclination, your preference. You could have been raised in an environment which stifled the development of this preference. Or it could have been a very positively reinforcing situation and you were encouraged to be who you are.

Remember, too, as we look at your preferences, that even though you are *mainly* one type or another, such as Extrovert vs. Introvert, that doesn't mean that your personality doesn't also incorporate some features of another type. Your preference or strength may be that of an Extrovert, but there will still be some of the Introvert in you.

Remember the word *preferences.* It's like being either left- or right-handed. Even though you may be left-handed, this doesn't mean you don't use your right hand. You just prefer your left. You may prefer it strongly or just a bit. You rely upon one hand more and gravitate to it. This will always be your preference. But the older you become the more you learn to use your non-preferred hand as well.

So let's consider who you are and who the other person is in your life. As you read the various statements to follow you will find that you agree with some, while others you won't relate to as much. Occasionally you may find yourself in both of the preference sets, but most of the time one will be predominant.[1]

Extrovert vs. Introvert

There are four pairs of preference possibilities in the Myers-Briggs structure. The first is Extroversion vs. Introversion.

Now, I'm sure you have your own definitions of what these mean, but it's important to be clear about them. This is the way people prefer to interact with the environment or to be energized. To generalize, an Extrovert (**E**) gains energy from people, while an Introvert (**I**) is energized by being alone. Remember that distinction as we offer further details.

E's: People Who Need People

E's (for Extrovert, remember) are social creatures. "People energy" is what they feed on. They're approachable by friends and strangers alike. Sometimes they may tend to dominate a conversation. Invite them to a six-hour party and they're on cloud nine. At the end of the party they're wired and ready to go out with friends for coffee at Denny's. They talk with everyone; in fact they may share too much too soon on a personal level.

E's are not the best listeners. For them, listening is harder than talking. They may also have a tendency to interrupt. If

≈ Extroverts have been described as walking mouths. They really have no idea what they're going to say until they hear themselves talking. ≈

they're dating an **I**, they might spend the evening answering their own questions, and then thank the **I** for a great time. If they're in a relationship, they tell others all about it. And they enter into relationships quite easily.

E's have been described as walking mouths. Instead of thinking first they talk first, and really have no idea what they're going to say until they hear themselves talking. They brainstorm out loud for the entire world to hear. The ideas they come up with aren't set in concrete. They're still working them out, but they let everyone else in on the process.

E's typically like noise. They look forward to the interruptions of phone calls, and if the phone doesn't ring they'll start calling people. When they come home, they'll turn on the TV and/or stereo even though they don't watch or listen. It's noise.

If E's are in a relationship, they become lonely when their partner isn't there. They look forward to doing things with their partner rather than just sitting around. You would think that E's are very secure, the way they connect with people; but they have a high need for affirmation and compliments from everyone, especially significant people. They may think they've done a good job, but they won't believe it until they hear it from someone else. They may ask you for your opinion, too.

I's and the Preference of Privacy

At the other extreme from E's, I's are drained by people. They need to "energize" during downtime or by being alone. Often they're seen as shy or reserved. They prefer to share their time with one other person or a few close friends. They are usually quiet among strangers. They love privacy and quiet time to themselves. They learn how to concentrate and shut out noise.

Invite I's to a six-hour party and they respond, "Six hours! You've got to be kidding. What will I do for six hours? I'd be wiped out!" So they go late, talk to selected people one at a time and leave early. That's comfortable for them.

I's are good listeners and hate to be interrupted when they talk. When they're in a relationship they tend to keep their thoughts to themselves and wish their partner would too, if he or she is an E. Also, I's tend to be cautious in entering into a new relationship.

I's need to formulate what they're going to say in the privacy of their minds before they're ready to share it. If pressured to give an immediate, quick answer, their minds shut down. They usually respond with, "Let me think about that," or "I'll get back to you on this."

When asked a question, I's usually take an average of seven seconds before responding. (The problem is, if the other person is an E, they usually wait about a second and a half before jumping in to give an answer.) I's wish other people would rehearse their thoughts as they do. They carry on great conversations with themselves, including what the other person said, then what they themselves said, what the other person said, etc. They can do this so realistically that they believe the conversation actually occurred. You can imagine what misunderstandings this could cause.

I's are suspicious of compliments. In turn they may be sparse in giving them. So if an I's partner is an E, what might this do to the relationship?

When I's are in a relationship, they can handle the other person being gone quite well. In a dating setting they may prefer just being with the other person, without a lot of activity and noise.

What about you? Do you see yourself as an E or an I? What about your partner? On the following graph, indicate where you see yourself by placing your initials there. Then indicate where you perceive your partner on the scale.

Introvert _____|_____ **Extrovert**

I's and E's Together?

Can an I and an E be compatible? What if they're extreme? You may assume that two I's and two E's would be more compatible because of their similarities. But other aspects of our personalities need to be factored in because they also play a part in the compatibility equation. Frankly, any two personality combinations take work.

A couple in which one is an E and the other an I may experience more excitement and romance in their relationship. The downside is they may have to work harder at being compatible. Those couples who have the same preference or who are closer together may find that compatibility comes more easily; but they will need to work on bringing stimulating ideas and resources into their relationship. If not, they could get into a rut!

The very factor that attracted the **E** and **I** to each other before marriage can be the major issue of conflict after marriage, as each person's preference will seem more extreme.

What can two different personality types do to be compatible?

1. Accept and verbally praise your partner's difference and uniqueness. Don't try to make him or her into a revised edition of yourself.
2. Praise God for the strengths in each preference, such as the **E**'s ability to connect socially and the **I**'s stability, strength and depth of thinking.
3. **E**'s need to remember that **I**'s can be exhausted by superficial socializing. They will prefer less frequent get-togethers with just a few people, particularly those they are comfortable with. An **E** can help in a large gathering of people by not introducing their partner to everyone, making them the center of attention, talking too loud, revealing personal items about their relationship, calling on them to pray out loud or asking them a question which requires an immediate response. An **E** could also single out for a partner individuals with whom he would be comfortable in a one-on-one conversation.

An **E** may want to ask her **I** partner to let her know when his battery has been drained and he needs to leave. **I**'s need to remember that their **E** partner thrives on being with people. Often they encourage their partner to get there before they do in order to have more time socializing.

I know one woman who married into a family of eight (that's right, *eight!*) strong extroverts. At family get-togethers she can last for about an hour. Then she takes a half-hour break by herself in another room to revitalize. You might think that's ridiculous or rude. No, it's reality—and the only way it can work. We can't fight the way God created us as unique beings. The other family members now understand the differences and accept this. You're looking for balance, as well as meeting one another's needs.

When I's hear their E partners brainstorming out loud, they shouldn't assume that they mean what they just said. They're just processing aloud for the whole world to hear. Just ask, "Are you brainstorming again?" and you'll probably hear a "Yes." On the other hand, it would be helpful for E's to announce that they are doing this when it occurs.

Some friends of ours are totally opposite. He's as much of an E as you can be, and she's an I. June doesn't say much in a group, but with close friends she talks more than Don. Don would love to have the house filled with people every Sunday afternoon. For June, three or four times a year is sufficient. How do they work this out? They have three couples over once a month after church. Two of the couples June knows and is comfortable with. The other couple is new to her, but in a small group she can get to know them. They've learned to be compatible.

What about you? What will you need to do to blend and grow? Remember, you can grow from these differences.[2]

Sensor vs. Intuitive

The next set of preferences has a profound impact on communication and intimacy in your relationship. They reflect what sort of information you gather, how you gather it and the way you pay attention to it. You're either what we call a Sensor or an iNtuitive.

S Is for Sensory Perceptors

If you are a Sensor, you're keyed into information that you receive through your senses. What you pay attention to are the facts and details of situations. This is what you perceive, or notice—it's what you believe.

What's it like being a Sensor (S)? It really shows up in communication. When you ask a question, you want a specific answer. If you ask your partner, "What time should I meet you?"

and she says, "Around four," that just won't do it. You may ask, "Does that mean 3:55, 4:00 or 4:05?" You're that literal.

If someone asks you if you have the time, you say "Yes"—but you don't tell them until they ask. You force others to be specific. You don't assume.

If you're an **S** and you're looking at something to purchase and your partner says, "It's a good deal. It's less than $100," that won't do, either. You want the bottom line. (Remember, the stronger your preference in this area, the more you are like this. If you're more toward the middle of the scale, the less intense you are.)

As an **S** you tend to be a focused person. You have a high level of concentration on what you're doing *now*—at the present. The future? Deal with it when it arrives. Don't waste time wondering what's next.

You're a doer. If you have a choice between sitting around thinking about something and performing a task, there's no question as to what you'll do. And you want to invest your efforts in tasks that yield results you can see.

You're a factual person. Theories don't thrill you, but good old facts do. This probably affects the type and style of preaching and teaching you respond to. When you hear something from another person you want it sequentially—A to B to C to D. You don't like it when others meander off the path.

S's have little use for fantasy. They wonder why people assume, speculate and imagine. What good does it do?

One of their biggest frustrations is when others don't give them clear guidelines or instructions. After all, they are very explicit and detailed when they tell someone something. So it really bothers them when they receive instructions that are just general guidelines.

They have difficulty seeing the overall plan of something because they focus in on what they're doing—they see the individual tree but not the forest.

When it comes to money (which can be a source for major conflict in a relationship) **S**'s are very exacting. Money to them is very tangible. When they have it they can use it, but only as much as the amount allows.[3]

The S's view of money is that it's a tool to be used. That's it. In a relationship they probably look at money realistically, rather than through rose-colored glasses.

Predictability in a relationship gives them a sense of security, whereas change throws them. As a relationship progresses and grows, they want to know where they stand. They want explicit signs of commitment such as formal announcements, rings, etc. They're open to hearing and considering others' input about a relationship, but they also have very clear roles and expectations for their relationships.[4]

N's and the Intuitive World

If your preference is iNtuition, the way you respond to the world is *not* through the five senses or by means of facts, but on the basis of your "sixth sense" or "hunches." Details and facts have

$\approx$ Intuitive people live for the future. Today? Its purpose is to help them get ready for tomorrow! $\approx$

their place (perhaps), but you can easily become bored with them. You don't take things at face value; instead, you look for the underlying meaning of relationships. You look for possibilities, and your focus is not on the here-and-now but the future.

N's are sometimes perceived as a bit absentminded. Why? Simply because they like to think of several things at once. Sometimes it's difficult to concentrate on what's going on at the moment because the future has so many intriguing possibilities. N's live for the future. Today? Its purpose is to help get ready for tomorrow!

N's have a unique way of dealing with time—to them it's relative. They may have a watch, but it doesn't help them be on time. "Late" doesn't register with them unless an event has started without them. They may also be late because they tried to do too much before they left.

Can you begin to see now how an **S** and an **N** might be attracted to one another? The staunch, staid, responsible one may admire the free-spirited butterfly. But can you also see the potential for driving each other up the wall with these same tendencies after the infatuation and honeymoon bliss wears off?

As **S**'s are seen as rock-stable persons, **N**'s are creative. Their minds seem always to be in motion figuring out things just for the fun of it.

Dr. Dave Stoop shares a choice example of the difference in the way an **N** and an **S** live life.

INtuitive people do things quickly. They start down the hill and soon find a ski jump. As they fly through the air, they land at the bottom of the hill. It took them less than a minute to get there, and they sit down and wait for their sensing spouses. When those people finally arrive, the intuitive people ask them, "What on earth took you so long?" After the sensing people relate all that they have seen on the way down the mountain, they stop and ask the intuitive people, "How did you get here?" INtuitive people can only say, "I don't know how, but I got here." Sensing people then reply, "It may take me longer, but at least I know how I got here." The sensing people see a lot of the details as well, whereas intuitive people are so quick to jump to a conclusion, they miss the details and sometimes miss out on the joy of the moment.[5]

Instead of accepting things at face value, **N**'s want to probe deeper, always asking, "Why is it this way?" They can drive an **S** crazy with their inquisitive, speculative nature, as with their general answers even to specific questions. **N**'s tend to see the forest rather than the individual trees, so specifics slip by them. On the other hand, even if they're sitting and looking at the forest they may not see it because their minds are elsewhere.

My wife Joyce (an **N**) and I (an **S**) may be watching a TV show and I'll comment about something we've just seen. (I think we both saw it.) Joyce will say, "Where was that?" It was right there in front of us. But something she saw triggered a thought that sent her mind careening off the subject, where she was figuring out and speculating about something else entirely! This is common.

It's difficult for others to follow an **N**'s directions and instructions because there's a vague quality to them.

And then there are finances! Balance your checkbook? What a chore. It's more intriguing to speculate how you're going to spend your next paycheck. Money creates opportunities, and who knows what doors it can open for you? **N**'s see the value of money in terms of its possibilities.

The way **N**'s figure out how much money they have is intriguing. They're very adept at rounding off...either way, up or down! Some **N**'s round *down* in their checking account any amount under 50¢ and round *up* any amount over 51¢. They have an exciting approach to money which may both intrigue and threaten an **S** at the same time.

N's tend to view relationships optimistically, at times even unrealistically. The subtle indications that a relationship is progressing are important—signs such as gifts, cards and remembering special dates. Change and variation in their relationship is very important. If others raise any concerns about their partner, they tend to turn a deaf ear. They spend time thinking about the ideal relationship and tend to overlook reality. They believe that the roles and expectations of a relationship are negotiable and open to change.[6]

It's interesting to note the differences between **S**'s and **N**'s when it comes to dating. For an **S** a date begins when you get together. Not so for an **N**. A date can start when the first arrangements are made. They think and fantasize about the date—and all the *possibilities*—for weeks. Once the date is over, they don't concentrate on that experience; they are already thinking about the next one. Actually what occurs in their imagination is better than the real thing. On the second date the **N** might describe the first date in such a way that the **S** wonders if they were on the same date. Reality can become a bit distorted by the imagination.[7]

What about you? Do you see yourself as an **S** or an **N**? What about your partner? On the following graph, indicate where you see yourself and where you perceive your partner to be.

Sensory   **iNtuitive**

How S's and N's Can Relate to Each Other

About 70 percent of our population are Sensors and 30 percent iNtuitives. What if you have a relationship with someone in the opposite camp?

As I indicated earlier, Joyce and I do. I'm an **S** and she's the **N**. We've learned to balance our relationship. The potential for conflict and misunderstanding is there. But so is a stronger relationship because of the unique contributions each of us makes to the other.

You may want to read back through the preceding description and note the various possibilities. Remember that an **S** would prefer the **N** to respond more like an **S**, and the **N** would prefer the **S** to be more like an **N**. You will need to do two things: learn how to flex and accomplish this to some degree, but also let the other person be, realizing that he or she is contributing something to you that you don't have. Here are some things to consider.

If you're an **S** and your partner is an **N**, your partner will challenge you with possibilities you've never considered. Be willing to consider them, instead of immediately responding with a negative response. Accept the fact that what the **N** does or says will probably raise your anxiety over the risk factor.

Sometimes **N**'s fail to notice something you've done for them, what you've served them, or new clothes or furniture. Let them know that it's important to you for them to notice and comment. And if you're an **N**, make it a point to do so.

If you're an **S**, you're *not* responsible for the **N**'s restlessness or discontent. You haven't caused it. And you can't fix it, either.

An **N** can be frustrated when an **S** isn't wildly enthusiastic about some of his dreams and ideas. But an **S** may be if the **N** presents them simply and factually, and suggests that his partner think about it. An **N** needs this in order to respond. Remember that your **S** partner will take care of routine details that you tend to overlook. Express your gratitude for this.[8] An **N** needs to remember that what is said to an **S** will be taken at face value. In other words, *literally.*

S's tend to use complete sentences when they speak, and they end these sentences with a period. It's definite. Emphatic. But **N**'s spin out sentences that omit certain information they assume the other person knows—and they end the sentence with a dash. They're tentative. So when these two types talk to one another, they listen to the other according to their specific trait and assume the other person is talking in the same way they talk.

An **S** husband asks his **N** wife if she'd like to go away to the mountains for the weekend. She says, "No...I don't think so—" He assumes that since she said "No," she meant it with a period. Not so! It was a dash. So when Friday comes, she asks her husband, "What time are we leaving for the mountains this weekend?"

He looks surprised and says, "What are you talking about? You said you didn't want to go!"

His wife replies, "I know I said that, but you should have known that's not what I meant. I needed to check on some things first, and I got them cleared up!"

Dr. Dave Stoop describes the iNtuitive mind as being in two parts. One part they're conscious of, and one part they're aware of but can't activate. It's like an iceberg—10 percent is above the water where it can be seen, 90 percent is underwater. The part they can't articulate won't pop to the surface for a couple of days or until someone helps them articulate it. Dave says,

It's important to know that you will never find out what the dash of the intuitive person means by asking a question. If that is what you do, you will simply get a rehash of the information that has already been given. Instead, the sensing person must paraphrase back to the intuitive person what he or she heard the intuitive person say, and then allow the intuitive person to add to what has been said already. And this paraphrasing needs to be repeated until the intuitive person says, "Yes, that's what I've been trying to say to you."

When intuitive people write out a first draft of a note or memo and then look at what they wrote, they will often add more information between the lines or up the side of the paper with an arrow to show where that thought goes. They do this because when they write, they can see the part of the iceberg that is still underwater.[9]

Unfortunately, both S's and N's often assume that their partner can read their minds. Major conflict is on the horizon unless these assumptions are dropped in favor of clarification.

When Joyce and I are having a discussion and I've heard an answer from her, I've learned to ask, "Now, is that with a period or a dash?" We laugh and then talk some more, and we relate to each other better by signaling this awareness.

When an S talks he usually identifies the topic and moves through it factually and sequentially, although a bit unimaginatively for an N. But an N may start talking without identifying the subject, give three or four sentences of background material, go around the barn twice because they tend to be tangential in their thinking, and then arrive at the subject. Can you imagine what the S is doing all this time?

Sometimes if you listen to two N's talking, neither finishes a sentence, but both know exactly what the other is talking about. It's amazing.

As an S, I've learned to add more possibilities and detail that Joyce, the N between us, would enjoy when I share. When she starts sharing but hasn't yet identified the topic, instead of getting frustrated as I used to I relax and realize I'm going to get the background information first and, when the subject is identified, I'll have the entire picture. It just won't be packaged the way I would—and that's all right. It's helped me become more flexible. On the other hand, Joyce works at identifying the subject in advance and letting me know she's switched topics. We're working together.

It's time for you to do some thinking. As we progress through these preferences there will be combinations which describe who you are in more detail. You now know about Extroverts and Introverts and about Sensors and iNtuitive personalities. But you could be a combination of these types—an **ES** or an **EN**. That would make a difference, wouldn't it? Or you could be an **IS** or an **IN**.

After reading the next chapter, you may want to return to the descriptions in this chapter, put your two preferences together, and reflect on what you are like with your unique combination.

Notes

1. For further understanding of personality types, the best resource is *Type Talk* by Otto Kroeger and Janet M. Thuesen (New York: Tilden/Delta, 1998).

2. Sandra Hirsh and Jean Kummerow, *Life Types* (New York: Warner Books, 1989), p. 16, adapted; Kroeger and Thuesen, op. cit., pp. 15, 16, adapted; David L. Luecke, *Prescription for Marriage* (Columbia, Md.: The Relationship Institute, 1989), pp. 54, 55, adapted.

3. Kroeger and Thuesen, op. cit., pp. 17, 18. Adapted.

4. Hirsh and Kummerow, op. cit., p. 30. Adapted.

5. Dr. David Stoop and Jan Stoop, *The Intimacy Factor* (Nashville: Thomas Nelson, Publishers, 1993), pp. 72, 73. Adapted.

6. Hirsh and Kummerow, op. cit., pp. 30, 31. Adapted.

7. Kroeger and Thuesen, op. cit., p. 127. Adapted.

8. Luecke, op. cit., pp. 58-60. Adapted.

9. Stoop and Stoop, op. cit., pp. 80, 81.

More About Personality Types: Decision-Making and Structuring

≈

How compatible are you and your partner when it
comes to making decisions and organizing your lives?
It can be all-out war or purposeful compatibility.

In this chapter, I want to outline two more personality preferences identified by the Myers-Briggs Type Indicator (MBTI) that
are also important indicators of compatibility, or of the need to
work at it harder. These categories reveal *Thinker* vs. *Feeler* preferences and *Judger* vs. *Perceiver* types.

Thinkers vs. Feelers

Do you ever struggle with making decisions? Or do you wonder
why and how your partner makes them so differently than you
do? Some people are Thinkers, who make decisions quickly,
while others are Feelers, who seem to take forever to reach a

decision. Some are very sharp, clear, definite and decisive, while others are cautious, gentle, investigative and option-oriented. For a relationship to succeed you will need to mesh your differences and develop your own decision-making style as a couple. This third set of MBTI preferences shows how you and your partner individually prefer to make decisions.

Dr. Dave Stoop describes these two personality types:

Thinking people can stand back and look at the situation. They make a decision from an objective viewpoint, interpreting the situation from the outside. They believe that if they gather enough data they can arrive at the truth. They are always searching for this truth, which they believe exists as an absolute. These people see things as black-and-white, as absolutes. If the answer seems to lie in the gray area, thinking people believe that they just haven't gathered enough data. If they can just look further, they will discover the truth.

On the other hand, feeling people always make decisions from a personal standpoint by putting themselves into the situation. They are subjective, believing that two truths can exist side-by-side.

The difference between a thinking person and a feeling person can be seen in the way the two make decisions, such as buying a car. Thinking people get the consumer reports and do research into different types of cars. They ask themselves, "Which is the best financial value? Which is safest?" They'll decide which criteria is most important to them and then make a decision based on that criteria. When they go to the car dealership, they'll know exactly what they want, and even that persuasive car salesman can't talk them into buying another car.

Feeling people start looking at all the cars on the road. "Which car would I like to be driving right now?" they ask themselves. "What color looks good? What make? What style?" When feeling people arrive at the car dealership, they may think, "I want a blue Honda coupe." But after they've looked around a while, they may fall in love with a metallic green Honda Accord. And that's the car they'll purchase—even if it costs more money.

The important questions to ask yourself are: How do I make a decision? Do I listen more to my head when I make good decisions, or do I listen more to my heart?

About two-thirds of women are on the feeling side, even though there is an equal distribution of both preferences in the American culture.[1]

The Thinking or Feeling preference is the trait that reflects how you *handle* your emotions, even though the trait really has very little to do with your emotions themselves. A Thinker (T) is often uncomfortable talking about feelings. They may also be uncomfortable in the area of aesthetics and building relationships. Other people may see them as aloof and cool, even though they are actually quite sensitive.

Feeling (F) individuals are comfortable with emotions. Not only are they aware of their own feelings, they can sense what others are experiencing as well. When it comes to making a decision, they're not just concerned with how it affects them but others as well.

To show you the difference, if a T were on a jury he would be concerned with justice and fairness. He'd look at the facts, find the truth, then make a decision. An F on a jury would be concerned with mercy. Facts are all right, but what were the circumstances? Why did the person do what he did? An F would want to give the benefit of a doubt.[2]

Do you have an idea yet where you stand on this? What about your partner? Are you comfortable with each other's traits? If you were to marry, how will your preferences impact you in five or 10 years? To help you answer these questions, let's consider each trait in detail.

Thinkers: Firm but Fair

If you're a Thinker (T), you're the one who stays calm and collected in a situation when everyone else is upset. You keep your wits about you.

You're the epitome of fairness when you make a decision. You're not that concerned with what will make others happy. You're more firm-minded than gentle-minded. You want to make sure others know where you stand, whether they like it or not. You'll state your beliefs rather than have others think they're right.

In fact, you're not concerned with whether people like you or not. What is important is being right. Your skin is quite thick. You can take it.[3] And argue? Sure—sometimes just for the fun of it. It's important for you to be objective even if others misinterpret you or your motives.

If you're a T you enjoy making hard decisions, and you can't understand why it's so difficult for others. Anything logical or scientific impresses you. You're drawn to it.

In your interpersonal relationships you have difficulty remembering names.

In a relationship you need logical reasons for the purpose of the relationship's even existing. The way you look at your partner is not only very realistic, but critical. You tend to correct and try to redefine your partner. This can be expressed both verbally and nonverbally.

T's are reserved in the way they show love, and sometimes it's quite impersonal. They don't want to be out of control.

T's have a built-in filter to screen out the emotional parts of communication. It's uncomfortable for them to share their emotions. The simple but important niceties in a relationship are lacking.[4]

Feelers and the Personal Dimension

If you're a Feeler (F) you're the person with an antenna sticking out that picks up how others are feeling. And sometimes you allow them to dictate how you respond. You tend to overextend yourself to meet the needs of others, sometimes even if it costs you.

In coming to a decision you're always asking, "How will this affect other people?" Sometimes you end up with a sense of tension—you like to help others, but sometimes you feel that you are always giving while others are taking. You may feel that others take advantage of you and that your own needs aren't being met.

If you're an **F** you are well-liked. Why? Because you're the peacemaker for everyone. "Let's all get along" is your motto. Sometimes others wonder if you have much of a backbone. You change what you've said if you think it's offended someone.

You are very aware of your personal reasons for a relationship. You see the best in your partner, and you don't hold back expressions of love. You show your caring in a very personal way through words, cards, actions, etc. You're constantly scanning the other person's messages to see if there's any emotional meaning to the words. Any offering of emotional response is appreciated—unless it's negative. You don't want anything to undermine your relationship.

T's and F's Together

One of the most typical relationships that develops is a **T**-male and **F**-female. This connection has the most potential for creating divisiveness and long-term problems. **T**'s need to think about and analyze their emotions. They bring to the relationship emotional control and reserve that can limit intimacy. They want to understand intimacy, not experience it, while **F** wants to share openly and experience intimacy.

If a couple doesn't learn to connect emotionally, they're at risk for either an affair or a marriage breakup. The bonding material of a marriage is emotional intimacy. **F**'s hunger for warmth, sharing and closeness, and without this dimension they can end up feeling lonely. They like the inner strength and security of a **T**, but not the perceived emptiness.

Unfair as it sounds, a **T** will need to work more in adapting than an **F**. Learning a vocabulary of intimacy and how to describe emotions is essential. A **T**'s uniqueness is definitely needed, but it can create a sterile relationship. **T**'s and **F**'s are attracted by each other's differences, but at the same time are a bit repelled by them. A **T** desires intimacy, but could fear it more.[5]

Feelers need to work on being less subjective, less responsible for everyone's emotional state. They need to take things less personally, to learn to become assertive and face disagreements. They need to stop saying, "I'm sorry" and "It's my fault" so much.

≈ Remember, you are and were attracted to each other because of who you both are. Each of you is incomplete without the other. You're a gift to each other. ≈

Well, what are you "thinking" or "feeling" right about now? Do you see yourself as a **T** or an **F**? What about your partner? On the following graph, place your initials where you see yourself, then write your partner's initials at the spot where you perceive him or her to be.

Thinker   **Feeler**

Working on Compatibility

Can a **T** and an **F** become compatible? Yes, but it will take constant work. You must avoid judging your partner for the way he is, and realize he will never become just like you. You can defeat yourself and put a strain on your relationship by trying to make your partner think like you. Sure a **T** wants the **F** to be more analytical and efficient and to get to the point quicker. The **F** wants more transparency, emotional expression and social awareness from the **T**. To a point both of you can learn to accommodate these desires. This is what is meant by learning to become compatible.

But both parties must remember that you are and were attracted to each other because of who you both are. See your partner's uniqueness as a gift and a plus for you. Look at it this way: Each of you is incomplete without the other. You're a gift to each other.

A **T** takes care of things, and an **F** takes care of people.

A **T** takes care of organization, and an **F** provides warmth and harmony.

A **T** brings emotional control to a relationship, while an **F** provides emotional energy.

A **T** gives structure, an **F** nurtures.

If you're a **T**, stretch yourself to enter into the social life provided by your **F** partner. Watch and listen to how **F**'s interact. When you're talking to one, be more expressive and tentative and use feeling words. You'll gain more friends that way. Accept the way your **F** partner shares. Praise your partner for her feelings, and tell her you need to learn what she has to offer.

Be realistic and accept the fact that you probably won't be able to satisfy all of your **F** partner's relational needs. Encourage her long, feeling conversations on the phone and her same-sex relationships. Don't force her to cut back on her friendships.

If you're an **F**, remind yourself of the qualities of your **T** partner. Note how you make use of his **T** characteristics. You'll need his problem-solving abilities. He will add energy, organization and direction to your spontaneity.

Remember that a **T** simply cannot fulfill all your social or relational needs. Don't interpret his cool reserve as personal rejection but as a personality trait. What may hurt you probably wasn't intended to hurt you. You may need to positively guide him in new ways to express things to you. But that's what relationships are all about—growth.[6]

Remember that both of you are a mixture of **T** and **F**. One trait is dominant in each of you, so you both may need to work on nurturing (I used a feeling word there because I'm an **F**) your less dominant preference.

By the way, when you pray for your partner, do you thank God for the fact that he or she is either a **T** or an **F**? That will do wonders.

Judgers vs. Perceivers

How do you like to live your life? Is it structured and organized, or is your approach to life free-flowing, spontaneous and adaptive? These traits are measured by the last MBTI category. People whose preference is structure are called Judgers, while free-form types are Perceivers.

This preference largely determines what you share when you begin to talk. Let's consider this in your steps to becoming compatible with your partner.

Judgers and the Quest for Order

If you're a Judger (J), you're very conscious of time and schedules. It's as though you have a built-in clock. You seem to spend a good portion of your life waiting for others who don't have a clear understanding of time. (By the way, how might a Judger view someone who is usually late?)

You're a list-keeper. You're probably one of those persons who has a Day-Timer and who makes it work. Crossing off listed items gives you great satisfaction. Your entire day is mapped out from the time you wake up until bedtime. If something interferes with your schedule, watch out.

In school you probably completed assigned projects in advance. And you do like order, from the way things are arranged in the cupboard to the color-coded clothes hanging a half-inch apart in the closet.

Your motto is, "Get the work done first, then you can play." If you have a task to do, you'll keep at it until it's done, even if waiting would give you better resources to do a better job.

J's view interruptions and surprises as totally unnecessary. People about them soon learn to tell them about a change that's coming, leave and let the J fuss for 10 minutes and get it out of their system, then come back to discuss it.

In order to be spontaneous, you have to plan it in advance! "A week from Sunday, I will be spontaneous from 1 to 5 P.M."

When you talk, you economize on words. You give decisions, but don't always provide enough data to back it up. (Can you imagine what it's like to live with a J who is also an Sensor and a Thinker?)

J's think of money as something that provides security. It's one of the ways to measure their success and progress. The best thing to do with money? Simple—save it. This means invest it wisely, budget it, be careful in giving it away, prioritize how to spend it, use it for your child's college and your retirement.

How do Judgers relate in a relationship? When they are certain of their feelings, they commit and then focus on getting the other person's commitment. They may even want to set up actual time periods to work on the relationship. They tend to put off the playful part of a relationship until work is out of the way. They know that one of the best ways to build a relationship is working together. They're comfortable with doing things traditionally or by the book in a relationship.

Perceivers and the Need for Spontaneity

Who do you think a J is often attracted to? You're right—a Perceiver (P). But talk about opposites! The Perceiver loves adventure—the unknown is there to be explored, even if it's finding alternative routes home each day. Planning is not for you. It's limiting. You would rather wait and see what unfolds.

Those who see you as disorganized just don't understand you. Neatness has little appeal for you. Sure, you would like to be organized, but that's not nearly as important as being *creative, spontaneous* and *responsive*. Can you see how these characteristics would both intrigue a J and frustrate him as well?

Time. What's time to a P? Even if you have a watch you don't look at it or want to be limited by it. You wait until the last minute to get things done, and although you usually get them done you upset others in the process. In school you probably pulled an all-nighter to get that paper done or to prepare for the exam.

As a **P**, your attention span is very flexible. That's another way to say you're easily distracted. You set out to another room to do something and end up in the garage doing something else.

Most everything you do turns into play. Things have to be "fun." If someone tells you that a work project will be fun, you respond positively.

It's difficult for you to make up your mind or to decide on something. If you do, it may limit you from doing something better that might come along. So others see you as noncommittal, hesitant or not having the ability to make up your mind.

You may come home with clothes from the store but take them back the next day because you'll find something better at another store. Being definite is not your forte. You don't want to rule out anything by deciding one way or another.

A P's motto is, "I'll get around to it," or, "It's around here somewhere."

When people ask you a question, you often respond with a question. You change the topic easily. (The word "ramble" comes to mind.) You can jump from one subject to another, and the topic may be something you saw through the window or a TV show you just watched.

You are very agile and flexible in your style of conversation. You don't need to resolve your discussions, even though you may go around the barn three or four times. When you make a point you may say it several different ways—it's as though you get paid by the word. But sometimes you're so vague that it's hard to follow your train of thought. If you're also an Extrovert, everyone will hear you change your thoughts in the middle of a sentence and even interrupt yourself.

It's an amazing experience for others to hear you talking with another **P** because the conversation can go anywhere and in all directions at one time. You may not finish your sentences before moving on, but the other **P** follows you. (A **J** wouldn't be able to.)

Then there's the way you look at finances. Money is a means to help you get the most out of life. The best way to use it is...*spend it!* Ask **P**'s what to do with money and you hear responses like: "Have fun with it." "Enjoy it when you have it." "If you see someone in need, give them some." "Take a trip on the spur of the moment." "Take some friends on a cruise."[7]

Perceivers experience some tension when considering commitment. They're more hesitant because they don't want to cut off other options. Sometimes they are up and down over the status of their relationships. When they do commit, it's still open for reevaluation.

Whereas a J wants security, a P wants freedom. This tendency is also seen in activities on the social calendar. A J wants to keep the appointment come what may, while a P says, "I may go and then again something else may come up that interests me more."

If there's work to do on the relationship, P's typically want to wait and deal with it when an issue arises. They'll look for ways to combine work and play. Traditional ways of responding in a relationship are restrictive. P's prefer to be creative, let it flow and see what develops.[8]

The differences between a J and a P in a relationship will be very evident, especially when dating, because these preferences are the most difficult to hide. On a date expect a J to take charge. If he's an E, you'll hear about it; but if he's an I it will happen. The date will be overplanned and scheduled. Rough plans don't work. A J is very goal-oriented when dating, while this may cause a P to feel confined, or even trapped. On a trip or extended time together, the differences become even more apparent, then extreme. As each falls back on his or her preferences, resentment can build.[9]

Well, where are you? Do you see yourself as a J or a P? What about your partner? On the following graph indicate where you see yourself by placing your initials there, then indicate where you perceive your partner.

Judging | **Perceiving**

J's and P's in Coexistence
How will you develop your compatibility in this situation? Here is what one author wrote about the task before you:

> Judging and perceiving organizers complement each other's styles. Judging people are sometimes tired of living in their structured, organized world and would love to break free. As they watch the play ethic of the perceiving

person, they long for that fun-loving approach to life. During the early stages of a relationship, they will often act a lot like the perceiving person, in that they will drop what they are doing and have some fun.

On the other hand, perceiving people get frustrated with always organizing and never actually being organized. They sometimes long for some structure in their lives or for someone who will be decisive and know where to put things. During the early stages of the relationship, they may even feel a spurt of organizational skill that puts some structure in their lives.

Judging people want some freedom from structure, but "not that much freedom." They begin to feel as if their lives are unraveling and they are losing control if things get too flexible, so they quickly go back to their strength and "tighten down the loose ends."

Perceiving people may look to their partner to help them get organized, but will begin to feel crowded by the seemingly endless structures and start to loosen things up a bit.

Of course, after we are in a committed relationship, we start to try to change the other person. As the focus begins to shift, judging people begin to look at perceiving people and think they are lazy and unorganized. Their play ethic feels like a character flaw, not a personality style. Instead of seeing them as playful, judging people begin to think of them as flaky and irresponsible. Perceiving people, who at first love the orderliness of judging people, become convinced they married someone who has an obsessive-compulsive disorder and may even suggest that the judging person get professional help.

One judging husband, who later admitted that what attracted him to his perceiving wife was her playful spirit, wanted to help her get organized. One weekend, when she was away visiting her family, he decided to make it easier for her to organize her kitchen. He emptied all the cupboards and the pantry, cleaned it all meticulously, and then put in new, white shelf-paper. As he put everything back into the cupboards, he took a black marker and made the shape of the item on the shelf-paper. Inside one circle, he wrote *peanut butter*. In a rectangle, he wrote *cereal*. He finished, of course, before she got home and couldn't wait for her appreciative response. After all, he was helping her get organized.

Little did he imagine the intensity of her reaction. She was livid! She took it as the ultimate insult. And for her it was, for he was saying that her personality style was inadequate, that she needed help. It didn't take very long for her to put the peanut butter where he had written *cereal* and the dishes over the word *glasses*.

Unfortunately this husband had lost sight of his appreciation of his wife's personality. When pressed, he could identify how much he enjoyed her spontaneity, her ability to manage a large number of things at one time, and her fun-loving spirit. Perhaps if he had shown her how much he appreciated these attributes she might have seen his organizational strength and asked him for help.

You might think that only judging people are perfectionists. The truth is that both types struggle with perfectionism. Perceiving organizers think they're great organizers, but if you ask them whether they can keep their files organized, they have to reply no. They are always in a hurry to get on to something else so they don't keep their things organized. These people often feel overwhelmed. They're always playing "catch up." Judging people are practicing perfectionists, and perceiving people are procrastinating perfectionists. For instance, a wife described how she struggled with her closet. She always was working on organizing it. One day, she got everything just the way she wanted it. She couldn't wait to show it to her husband. And he was truly impressed, it looked great.

They got into a fight, however, when he walked out of the closet and saw the "piles" of things that didn't fit into the closet, lying on the bedroom floor. He made the mistake of asking her what she intended to do with them. He was afraid that as soon as someone came to visit, the piles would quickly go back into the closet again, and all of his wife's work would go down the drain. Of course he forgot that she never did claim to be able to maintain the closet, she was simply "always organizing it."[10]

If you are a J or a P trying to connect with your opposite, consider the strength each of you brings to the relationship. A P is the one who expands information and alternatives before decisions are made. Some of these could be better than what the J partner has considered. The J will see that conclusions are reached and the decisions followed.

Each of you will need to give more time in order to hear what the other has to say. Don't immediately think the other is wrong or try to convince him that you're right. Don't engage in labeling. (P's tend to call J's closed-minded, opinionated and stubborn, whereas J's are tempted to label P's flaky, unsupportive or wishy-washy.)

Avoid competition.

J's can encourage P's to take more time, consider alternatives, change their mind. They can also work on being less definite and emphatic when they make statements. They can give in to the other person, and instead of always giving advice or conclusions, ask a question.

J's can give their P partners more responsibility for planning and decisions. Don't expect them to immediately back your decisions. They need time to explore. Don't back the P into a corner by predetermining responses and solutions. J's must stretch their ability to live with unanswered questions, things being out of control and indecision.

If you are a J, remember that there is more than one right answer. Don't take a P's apparent lack of commitment and support personally. She has a different timetable and intensity. Remember that her motto is, "I'll get around to it," and even that will be voiced tentatively.

Both of you, J and P alike, should purposefully do things the way the other does every now and then. It will help you flex. And you may be surprised that you can do it.[11]

Thank each other for the way you are. You need what each other has to offer. You may just be threatened by differences.

If you're a **P**, above all make every effort to be on time when you have told your J partner you would be there. We live in a society that puts value on punctuality. You could write yourself some reminder notes and place them where you can see them easily and frequently.

Sometimes **P**'s think they can get "just these four tasks completed" before they leave, and that contributes to their being late. The way to overcome this is to come up with the four things you think you can do, then do just one or two of them. You could probably finish these, feel good about it and still be on time. Perhaps you need to begin seeing yourself as a person who *is* on time!

As a **P**, be more definite when you share how you feel about your partner. Let him know you're not challenging his decisions. You just need time to explore on your own. Keep in mind that what your J partner is saying may not be set in concrete, even if he says it is. Ask your partner how important a decision is on a scale of 0 to 10; and if it's anything more than a 6, follow through on it.

If you tend to drift off the topic in a conversation and your J partner brings you back to the issue at hand, thank him for doing so. You probably needed that.[12]

Remember that your J partner's need for certainty and structure is who he is, not a personal vendetta to control you.

Putting It All Together

I've talked to numerous couples who believe that they have an ideal relationship because they both have the same set of preferences on the Myers-Briggs. Perhaps, but maybe not. The combination of your preferences does affect your marriage, but both the preferences you have and the ones you don't have help determine the quality of your relationship.

You may have a complementary advantage when you have the same preference, but lack the advantage of the one you're missing. For example, if both of you are missing a certain preference, you would probably avoid the activities or experiences enjoyed by someone with that preference. You would have to make an effort to access your non-preference side and learn to use it. You will need to read as much as you can about the missing preferences and learn to compensate for what you don't have.

Let's look at each preference and see what you may need to do.

If both of you are Sensors (S) then you may miss out on the joys an iNtuitive (N) personality can bring to life. Where's the fantasy? Where are the imaginative possibilities? You may be too problem-oriented and too limited in your thinking. You may need the impact of others to stimulate your minds in new directions.

If you're both Introverts (I), who is going to be the one who initiates social life? Probably no one. You could end up being a bit bored with each other if you lack the social contacts that come naturally to an Extrovert (E). And how much will you talk to each other? You may need to structure times to talk together. You could plan to get together with others once a week just to force yourselves to interact with them.

On the other hand, if you're missing Introversion because you're both Extroverts, you may rob yourselves of the advantage of quiet times and solitude. You could end up burning out because you lack someone to help slow you down. What can you do? Plan some time alone each week for reading, relaxing or just being quiet.

If you're missing the Sensory dimension because you're both iNtuitives, watch out! You may need help with a reality check! You may lack the necessary attention to details such as your budget, home repairs and auto maintenance. You may need to identify what it is you don't like doing, then divide up the tasks. Sure, you like to play—so discover the play aspect of dealing with the details of life.

If you're missing Thinking because you're both Feelers, you

may have a hard time getting to solutions because you both focus on the emotional perspective. And you may try too hard to please each other. A missing ingredient is the capacity for rational problem-solving. Delay some of your emotional responses to access your thinking side. Ask yourself, "How would a **T** respond to this?"

If you're missing Feeling because you're both Thinking, where's your empathy? Others may see you as an uncaring couple. You also may be sparse in giving compliments and appreciation. You can learn a Feeling vocabulary. Give at least one compliment a day and ask yourself, "How might a Feeling person respond to this?"

If you're missing Judging because you're both Feelers, chaos could be the theme of your life. Your home could reflect lots of projects started, but not completed. If planning escapes you, you may find yourself overloaded and out of control. So keep a calendar and be sure all activities are placed on it. Practice completing a project so you can experience the satisfaction.

If you're missing Perceiving because you're both Judgers, you will tend to over-structure your life and miss the "Two P's"— Possibilities and Play. You may make things too much like work. Rigidity may be your byword. Learn to enjoy. Purposely try new things. Become a risk-taker.[13]

Hopefully you now have a better understanding of yourself and your partner. I would encourage you again to read the book *Type Talk* by Otto Kroeger and Janet M. Thuesen. It is much more detailed than this presentation, describing not only each MBTI type but the 16 combinations of preferences as well.

For example, what if you're an ENFP and your partner is an ESIJ? How will you get along? What will it take to learn to be compatible?

You may look at all of this and ask, "Is this necessary? It looks like a lot of work!" Or you could look at it and say, "Look at all the possibilities. This could be fun!" Of course, how you respond will not only make a significant difference in your relationship. It will also reflect your personality type preference, won't it?

Notes

1. Dr. David Stoop and Jan Stoop, *The Intimacy Factor* (Nashville: Thomas Nelson Publishers, 1993), pp. 88, 89.
2. Ibid., pp. 90, 91. Adapted.
3. Otto Kroeger and Janet M. Thuesen, *Type Talk* (New York: Tilden/Delta, 1998), pp. 18, 19. Adapted.
4. David L. Luecke, *Prescription for Marriage* (Columbia, Md.: The Relationship Institute, 1989), pp. 44, 45. Adapted.
5. Ibid., p. 43. Adapted.
6. Ibid., pp. 64-69. Adapted.
7. Kroeger and Thuesen, op. cit., pp. 21, 22, adapted; Otto Kroeger, *16 Ways to Love Your Love* (New York: Delacorte Press, 1994), pp. 86, 87. Adapted.
8. Luecke, op. cit., p. 59. Adapted.
9. Kroeger and Thuesen, op. cit., pp. 132, 133. Adapted.
10. Stoop and Stoop, op. cit., pp. 112-115.
11. Luecke, op. cit., pp. 71, 72. Adapted.
12. Kræger, *16 Ways to Love Your Love*, p. 97. Adapted.
13. Sandra Gray Bender, Ph.D., *Recreating Marriage with the Same Old Spouse* (Louisville, Ky.: Westminster/John Knox Press, 1997), pp. 80, 81. Adapted.

Concluding Thoughts:

Tying It All Together

≈

Relationships that work—they do exist. And there is one last ingredient that will draw it all together for you. I haven't mentioned it yet, but it's time:

Where are you in your relationship with Jesus Christ?

And if you are dating someone, where is this person spiritually?

You can take everything else I've already said and put it to the side while you consider the dimension of spiritual togetherness.

Keep this in mind: When each person in a relationship has a personal commitment to Jesus Christ as Lord and Savior of his and her life and are openly seeking to serve Him, this couple has a foundation that will stay with them throughout the years of their marriage.

The spiritual dimension can't be something that is tacked on as an afterthought. The relationship is built upon a spiritual foundation. When there is spiritual incompatibility in a relationship or marriage, the result is a hole in the center of the couple's life together. There is an emptiness in that segment of life. There is no real connection in the most important aspect of their relationship.

The spiritual dimension affects other dimensions of the relationship. Your social life will be impacted, as there will be activities and friendships one partner could care less about than the other. Your intellectual growth in the spiritual realm will be a solitary endeavor since one of you will have no desire to learn. And since a close spiritual relationship has such a positive effect upon the sexual dimension in a marriage, the physical won't be all it could be.

When you become interested in another person, explore the spiritual level of that person as soon as possible. Continue to explore it and observe its growth. All too frequently I have seen one person misrepresent themselves, proclaiming to the other what they actually were not spiritually. For example, the man may say that he is "not against religion" or "not an immoral person" or "not opposed to your spiritual growth." This feigned interest is part of the plan to present an attractive package to the other person.

You may be seeing someone who states that he is a Christian. But you need an affirmative answer to these three questions to realize your marriage potential.

- Is the other person (and are you) reflecting a desire to continue growing in Jesus Christ?
- Is there an observable difference today spiritually with either of you as compared with six months ago?
- Do both of you have a similar understanding and acceptance of biblical values?

Spiritual intimacy in a marriage is cultivated before the marriage vows occur. Begin now. Being able to share your spiritual self will draw you closer together. Remember that sharing is something you both do. It's a step of disclosing some of your most personal values. You may share your beliefs, your insights, even your unbeliefs. It's a step of being willing to seek God's guidance together, to allow the teaching of His Word to influence your dating relationship. It's a willingness to enthrone Jesus Christ as Lord of your lives and to look to Him for all decisions.

Some couples seem to be able to develop spiritual intimacy, while others never do. What makes the difference? Spiritual intimacy has the opportunity to grow in a relationship that has a degree of stability. When the two of you experience trust, honesty, open communication and dependability, you are more willing to risk being vulnerable spiritually. Creating this dimension will increase the stability factor as well.

For you to have spiritual intimacy you need shared beliefs as to who Jesus is, and agreement on the basic tenets of the Christian faith. You may have different beliefs about the second coming of Christ, or whether or not all the spiritual gifts are for today. One of you may enjoy an informal church service, while the other likes a high-church formal service. One of you may be charismatic and the other may not be. There can still be spiritual intimacy within such diversity, if each of you realizes and respects that your beliefs are basic to who you are. You've made them something personal and significant to your life.

We hear about mismatched couples when one is a Christian and one isn't. You can also have a mismatch when both are believers but one wants to grow and is growing, and the other doesn't and isn't.

One way to develop both your relationship and your spiritual intimacy is to share the history of your spiritual life. Many couples know where the other person is currently, but very little of how they came to that place. Discuss together the following questions to discover how your faith compares with that of your partner:

1. What did your parents believe about God, Jesus, church, prayer and the Bible?
2. What is your definition of being "spiritually alive"?
3. Which parent did you see as being spiritually alive?
4. What specifically did each parent teach you directly and indirectly about spiritual matters?
5. Where did you first learn about God? About Jesus? About the Holy Spirit? At what age?
6. What was your best experience in the church as a child? As a teen?
7. What was your worst experience in church as a child? As a teen?

8. Describe your conversion experience. When and where was it? Who was involved?

9. If possible, describe your baptism. What did it mean to you?

10. Which Sunday School teacher influenced you the most? In what way?

11. Which minister influenced you the most? In what way?

12. What questions did you have as a child/teen about your faith? Who gave you any answers?

13. Did any camp or special meetings affect you spiritually?

14. Did you read the Bible as a teen?

15. Did you memorize any Bible passages as a child or teen? Do you remember any now? Do you memorize Scripture currently?

16. As a child, if you could have asked God any questions, what would they have been?

17. As a teen, if you could have asked God any questions, what would they have been?

18. If you could ask God any questions now, what would they be?

19. What approach to spirituality would have helped you more when you were growing up?

20. Did anyone disappoint you spiritually as a child? If so, how has that impacted you as an adult?

21. Did you go through any difficult times as a child or teen that affected your faith?

22. What has been the greatest spiritual experience of your life?

23. What Christian books have you read in the last five years?

24. Describe your devotional life at the present time.

Suppose that these questions have revealed glaring fundamental differences between you and your partner. What will you do with this information? As painful as reexamining your relationship may be, it is nothing to the agony of realizing after marriage that you are worlds apart.

When Scripture states, "Be ye not unequally yoked together with unbelievers" (2 Cor. 6:14, *KJV*), it is quite clear about whom you should marry. When Paul compares the relationship between husband and wife to that between Christ and His Church (Eph. 5:21-33), it is apparent that this analogy is referring to both individuals knowing the Lord.

A clear-eyed vision of the significance of spiritual compatibility is so much more important than romantic urges—if both of you are committed to a fulfilling relationship and to the lordship of Christ.

Appendix I

Preparing for the Next Marriage

≈

Or How Not to Repeat the Mistakes of a Previous Marriage

(Permission granted to make a single photocopy of this section for your partner.)

I. Describe your expectations for your new marriage:

_____

_____

_____

_____

_____

_____

_____

_____

_____

II.   What was your former marriage like? Let's compare it with your new prospective partner.

    1. a. How long did you know your previous spouse before you began to date?

        b. How long did you know your current partner before you began to date?

    2. a. What attracted you to your former spouse?

        b. What attracted you to your current partner?

    3. a. How long did you date your former spouse before deciding to marry?

        b. How long did you date your prospective spouse before deciding to marry?

    4. a. What were your reasons for wanting to marry your former partner?

        (1)

        (2)

        (3)

        (4)

        (5)

        b. What are your reasons for considering marriage to your current partner?

(1) _____

(2) _____

(3) _____

(4) _____

(5) _____

5. What dream did you have for your prior marriage?

_____

_____

_____

_____

_____

6. What dream do you have for your pending marriage?

_____

_____

_____

_____

_____

III. Characteristics and personality traits

1. List 10 adjectives that describe your former spouse.

(1)_____   (6)_____

(2)_____   (7)_____

(3)_____   (8)_____

(4)_____   (9)_____

(5)_____   (10)_____

2. List 10 adjectives describing your prospective spouse.

(1) _____   (6) _____

(2) _____   (7) _____

(3) _____   (8) _____

(4) _____   (9) _____

(5) _____   (10) _____

Now indicate with a check mark the adjectives in both lists that describe you.

3. *Underline* any of the following descriptions that apply to you. Place a *check mark* by any that apply to your former spouse. *Circle* any that apply to your prospective spouse.

Perfectionistic tendencies	Overworks	Sleeps too much
Compulsive behavior	Procrastination	Difficulty at work
Type A behavior	Smokes	Insomnia
Risk-taker	Suicidal threats	Crying
Impulsive behavior	Suicidal behavior	Use of pornography
Loss of control	Withdraws from others	Aggressive behavior
Use of drugs	Worry	Verbally abusive
Use of alcohol	Depression	Physically abusive
Overeats	Low self-esteem	Lazy

4. Describe the pattern of marital satisfaction in your previous marriage, filling in the appropriate months or years on the bottom line of the scale.

High |

Medium |

Low |

First year   End of Marriage

    a.   Indicate on the chart when the conflicts started, what they were about and how they manifested themselves.

    b.   What did you do to improve the relationship?

_____

_____

_____

    c.   Indicate on the chart when the decision to divorce was made, and who decided.

    d.   How long did the divorce process take?

_____

    e.   Describe in detail how your divorce has impacted and changed you.

_____

_____

_____

_____

_____

f.   What will you bring into this next marriage from the previous marriage?

_____

_____

_____

_____

_____

g.   What do you *not* want to bring to your next marriage and how will you avoid this?

_____

_____

_____

_____

_____

5. Describe the pattern of marital satisfaction you predict you will have in your new marriage:

High

Medium

Low

   1st year   2nd year   3rd year   4th year   5th year

Now describe specifically what you will do to make this a reality:

_____

_____

_____

_____

_____

_____

_____

6. In what way is your present relationship similar to the former one?

_____

_____

_____

_____

_____

7. In what way is your present relationship different from the former one?

_____

_____

_____

_____

IV. Now compare the expectations you listed at the beginning of this questionnaire with these realistic expectations of any second marriage:[1]

1. You can expect it to be tougher than a first marriage.

2. You can expect it to be complicated, exasperating and tiring.

3. You can expect it to be a slow building process.

4. You can expect some "same old script" times, but know that you are writing a new script each day.

5. You can expect to want to run from it every now and then—but you won't.

6. You can expect a lot of outside pressures that are new to you. They come from parents, children, families, jobs and former spouses.

7. You can expect your second marriage to be successful if

you dig in and go for the long haul instead of the overnight wonder.

8. You can expect frequent visits from the ghosts of your previous marriage, but a good blast of reality will make them disappear.

9. You can expect *not* to become a "second-marriage failure" statistic.

10. You can expect not to run when the going gets tough, nor do you intend to serve a sentence called "marriage." You can expect to solve the problems that cause the "run or rust" mentality in a second marriage.

11. You can expect this marriage to be different because you have learned many things from the failure of your first marriage.

12. You can expect this marriage to become a "working model" for all to watch and encourage.

Note
1. From Jim Smoke, *Growing Through Remarriage* (Grand Rapids: Fleming H. Revell, 1990), pp. 90, 91. Used by permission.

Appendix II

Results of Living Together

≈

Cohabitation, or "living together," is an experimental family lifestyle that has increased dramatically in popularity over the last two decades. With an increase in this type of relationship of more than 700 percent since 1970, it is time to look back and ask, What are the effects of living together upon marriage and relationships?

1. The expectation of a positive relationship between living together and marital stability have been shattered. Studies from the United States, Canada, Sweden and New Zealand show the divorce rates substantially higher for those who cohabitate than those who don't. The differences range from 50 to 100 percent higher! Forty percent of those who live together break up, and those that marry have a 50 percent higher divorce rate than those that don't.
2. Those who live together have less healthy relationships than those that don't. They have lower relationship quality, lower stability and a a higher level of disagreements.
3. Those who live together are more violent than those who don't. The rate of violence is twice as high, and the rate for "severe violence" is almost five times as high for cohabitating couples compared to married couples.

4. Women in cohabitating relationships have much higher rates of depression than those in marriages. They also have more anxiety about their relationships than married women.[1]

Cohabitation has not delivered on its promise!

Note

1. See Glenn T. Stanton, *Why Marriage Matters: Reasons to Believe in Marriage in Postmodern Society* (Colorado Springs: Pinon Press, 1997).